Monster guic

to jobhunting

Monster guide
to jobhunting

Get the perfect job, **double click**

Andrew Chapman

An imprint of **Pearson Education**

London • New York • San Francisco • Toronto • Sydney • Tokyo • Singapore
Hong Kong • Cape Town • Madrid • Paris • Milan • Munich • Amsterdam

PEARSON EDUCATION LIMITED

Head Office:
Edinburgh Gate
Harlow CM20 2JE
Tel: +44 (0)1279 623623
Fax: +44 (0)1279 431059

London Office:
128 Long Acre
London WC2E 9AN
Tel: +44 (0)20 7447 2000
Fax: +44 (0)20 7240 5771
Website: www.business-minds.com

First published in Great Britain in 2001

© Pearson Education Limited 2001

The right of Andrew Chapman to be identified as author of this work has been asserted by him in accordance with the Copyright, Designs and Patents Act 1988.

ISBN 0 273 65409 8

British Library Cataloguing in Publication Data

A CIP catalogue record for this book can be obtained from the British Library.

10 9 8 7 6 5 4 3 2 1

Designed by Claire Brodmann Book Designs, Lichfield, Staffs
Typeset by Northern Phototypesetting Co. Ltd, Bolton, Lancs
Printed in Great Britain by Biddles Ltd, Guildford and King's Lynn

The Publishers' policy is to use paper manufactured from sustainable forests.

About the author

Andrew Chapman is a freelance writer, editor and designer working across a peculiar variety of fields, from the internet and recruitment to medicine, religion and property. After graduating from Edinburgh University and spending an unlikely spell as a security guard, he went to work for Future Publishing, where at the age of 23 he became an editor of one of its computer magazines.

Since then he has freelanced for a wide range of titles, including *The Independent*. He is an associate editor of *Interviewer*, the leading weekly news magazine for the recruitment industry, and he has also been closely involved with the launch of numerous websites. He is now developing an entirely impractical website of his own.

If you have any comments about this book or want advice on how to become a security guard yourself, Andrew can be contacted via one of his many electronic aliases: *goldwatch@thoughtplay.com*.

About the other people

I would like to thank everyone who has contributed to this book in any way, even by their absence, and I warmly appreciate the assistance from all those I have mercilessly harangued by e-mail. I dedicate the section on 'information overload' to them.

Special thanks must go to Ben Giddings, UK content and product manager of Monster.co.uk, who has helpfully co-ordinated a number of those contributions and offered his valuable expert advice, and to Amanda Thompson, Vivienne Church and Linda Dhondy for bringing the manuscript kicking and screaming into the light of day.

I am grateful, too, to the Starcats, Pablissimo, Mr Flip and Slip the Bridle, as well as to all my friends and family who have helped me to see around corners.

Finally, I would particularly like to thank Rachael Stock and Rosalind Renshaw, without whom, for me, none of this would have been possible.

This book is dedicated to Junior, wherever you are.

Contents

CONTENTS

CHAPTER SEVEN

Testing times Prepare yourself **for scrutiny**

CHAPTER EIGHT

Face to face ... but maybe apart

CHAPTER NINE

You can always improve

CONTENTS

Chapter summaries

Preface

What this book is all about, who should read it, what it will and won't tell you, and how it works.

Chapter 1 – Why am I here?

The role of the internet in jobhunting, and what sort of services you can expect to find.

Chapter 2 – Be a hunter-gatherer

Using the internet to research job markets and companies, and how to get the best out of search engines.

Chapter 3 – Bring it on

Using search agents to bring job vacancies to your desktop, and how to get the matches you really want.

Chapter 4 – Shop around

Expand your horizons through niche recruitment sites, teleworking, working abroad, or using new technology such as WAP and digital TV.

Chapter 5 – Meet the people

Get in touch with the experts through online forums, newsgroups, mailing lists and chatrooms.

Chapter 6 – Applying yourself

The secrets of good covering letters and CVs – on the net and on paper.

Chapter 7 – Testing times

How to approach psychometric tests, and how to use them to your advantage.

Chapter 8 – Face to face ... but maybe apart

How to prepare for interviews in person, by phone, across the internet or by videoconference.

Chapter 9 – You can always improve

Using the net to make the most of the job you've got, and to learn new skills through online training.

Chapter 10 – Striving and arriving

Answers to common fears, misconceptions and misunderstandings about the internet.

Preface

n days of yore when you'd had enough of your job – although it was a job for life, of course – the traditional path to finding another lay in holing yourself up in the corner of a greasy spoon with a red Biro and a stack of newspapers. Or if you were brave, and didn't mind being interrogated by strangers, you'd walk into a recruitment agency and they'd thoughtfully find you something else you didn't want to do. Or perhaps you'd tug the old school tie – and find yourself being strangled.

Those days are gone, up to a point. The newspapers are still there, and many jobs are filled in this way. But the same papers are now putting all their job ads on the internet, where you can search through them in moments rather than cholesterol-fuelled hours, and the only hazard is destroying the keyboard with a splash of café latté. The recruitment firms meanwhile are either entrenched in defending their old way of life or going online like everyone else. And who wants to wear a tie of any kind?

If you're reading this book, the chances are that you're online yourself in some way – sending e-mails from work and perhaps also from home, using the web to read the news or book a train ticket. Although folk in the US may look down on us, we are catching up, and the internet really is part of everyday life.

We have yet to embrace using it for everyday tasks with wholehearted enthusiasm, however, and people are often vague about using it – or they are misled.

This book is not a guide to getting online, or indeed a directory of sites to check out when you're there, although if you follow its guidelines you'll come across plenty and examples are often mentioned in passing. It's the *Monster* guide to jobhunting, of course. This does not mean that the book is a shameless advertisement for one particular company, nor that you are in any way being steered away from looking at others. What it does mean is that it has been written with the guidance of real experts. Monster.co.uk is inevitably used as an example of how that particular kind of site works, and it's a leader in its field. But there are others. Good sites speak for themselves.

There's also little point in listing sites *en masse* – web addresses often change, they die and rise again, usually with a Flash movie added to the home page. What you need to know is how to find them for yourself. So it's plainly and simply a guide to looking for new job opportunities, maximising your chances of getting them and hopefully finding some excellent careers advice while you're there. What it will tell you is how to do that on the internet, but never to the exclusion of other methods, however convenient the internet may be.

You will find advice on how to use your PC (or Mac or whatever) effectively in the job-hunting process, which includes some technical tips, but you will not find anything on how to sign up to a service provider, or what speed modem to buy. That's up to you, and there are far too many people offering conflicting advice on these things already.

The assumption is that you are generally aware of the internet but don't consider yourself an expert, and probably don't particularly feel inclined to become one. You have a need – to find a new job, or perhaps to develop your skills in your present one – and you just want to pick up the tools, be told what to do with them, and get on with it.

The internet has not replaced other forms of jobhunting, but it is a valuable supplement to them. So valuable, in fact, that you really will be missing out if you don't use it.

Who should read this book:

☞ anyone looking for a new job, in any field;

☞ anyone wanting to change their career;

☞ anyone wanting to develop their skills in the workplace.

What this book will tell you:

☞ how to use the internet as an effective jobhunting tool;

☞ how to use the internet as an efficient means of gathering information;

☞ how to make the whole jobhunting process more rewarding and enjoyable.

What this book won't tell you:

☞ how to buy the right computer;

☞ how to connect to the internet;

☞ how to suck eggs.

How the **book works**

Each section of this book is intended to be a straightforward and practical exploration of a particular stage or aspect of the jobhunting process, from vague dissatisfaction at your desk to shaking hands with your new boss. General advice on jobhunting will be offered, but only where it illuminates the purpose of this process using the internet.

The first chapter will introduce the scope of what is already possible for the internet jobhunter and invite you to try things out straight away. Most chapters contain a few simple, practical exercises – these are here to help you get a real flavour of what's possible, and you are urged to see for yourself. The book also divides into two halves, the first (Chapters 2–5) looking at finding job opportunities and the second at how to get somewhere with them.

Throughout the book there are panels offering at-a-glance information: on using search engines effectively, for example, or tips on building an online CV. Sometimes they offer quick reminders on more traditional ways of doing things, too.

On some pages you will also find 'hyperlinks', which offer relevant cross-references within the book to help you follow a particular train of thought – which, of course, is one of the unique advantages of the internet itself. Further references to particular topics can usually be found in the index.

This 'hypertext' approach means that you can read any chapter at any time and still get to the advice you want – the plot is written by you. I hope it has a happy ending.

CHAPTER ONE

Why am I here?

The ins and outs **of the internet**

Jobhunting is more than simply looking for vacancies or even finding out about the type of jobs you can do: it's also about finding out about yourself

At the time of writing, estimates suggest that in the UK alone around 4 million people are already using the internet in some way or other to aid their search for a new job (*source:* Workthing). By the end of 2001, this figure is likely to have doubled, representing about 14 per cent of the population. In 2000, 88 per cent of final-year graduates were actively using the net in preparation for launching into a career (*source:* Association of Graduate Recruiters) and two-thirds of graduate employers are now recruiting through the internet. About a third of British people have internet access either at home or at work, and digital TV looks set to boost that figure dramatically.[1]

'Using the internet' or 'being online' are broad phrases, but although the terms are often identified with the world wide web, there are many different parts to it. Using the internet to aid jobhunting can mean many things, including:

1 How is digital TV going to offer new jobhunting opportunities? **page 69.**

- ☞ sending enquiries or application letters by e-mail;[2]

- ☞ creating a CV[3] to be sent as an e-mail attachment;[4]

- ☞ signing up to an electronic mailing list[5] or newsletter;

- ☞ using a jobsearch database;[6]

- ☞ posting a message on a bulletin board or forum;[7]

- ☞ asking questions of an expert in an online chat session;[8]

- ☞ downloading a PDF application form;[9]

- ☞ calling someone via internet telephone;[10]

- ☞ reading or posting to a newsgroup about a particular industry or interest;[11]

- ☞ doing an online personality test.[12]

You will encounter many more examples in the course of this book. The point is that whatever your perception of the internet as a valuable tool in everyday life situations, you are quite likely to be using it already if you're working in an office environment, or in research or academia, and indeed if you just want to keep in touch with friends around the country or abroad.

So the assumption is that at some point in recent months you've sent an e-mail or looked up some information on the web – these are the bread-and-butter facilities that most people find most useful, most of the time. But even if you consider yourself a dab hand at all this, the chances are that there's still a lot more you can achieve using just these two aspects of the internet alone.

There's much more to play with, however, and the aim of this book is to introduce you to that broader scope. The central message is that there's no substitute for trying things, and you've really got nothing to lose. Everyone has concerns about security of personal

2 How do I write an e-mail covering letter? **pages 98, 102, and 108.**
3 Are online CVs any different from traditional paper ones? **page 38, page 103.**
4 What format should I send attachments in? **page 104.**
5 What's a mailing list? **page 83.**
6 How do I set up an effective jobsearch? **page 36.**
7 How do online message boards work? **pages 73–77.**
8 What's the correct way to communicate in a chatroom? **page 89.**
9 What is PDF? **page 105.**
10 How do I make phone calls using the net? **page 133.**
11 What are newsgroups? **page 78.**
12 Are there any serious personality tests online? **pages 114–117.**

data,[13] viruses,[14] junk mail[15] and so on, but if you observe simple rules and respect the medium, there's really nothing to be afraid of.

_____ The internet **imperative** _____

Many 'traditional' businesses have taken a certain smug satisfaction as legions of recently launched dot coms have flourished and fallen, and the prophets of doom have warned that the whole e-boom has been an e-bubble. For some firms leaping on to a bandwagon without the momentum to stay on it and get somewhere, this is probably true. But from now on it's safer to assume that the internet is always with us.

We can also assume two general principles at work:

☞ key players will emerge from the fallout bigger and stronger than before;

☞ whatever can be done will be done, and the scope of what can be done is always growing.

In the first case, thinking of the recruitment sector in particular, it's already clear that any serious-minded firm which has been running an internet jobs service for more than four years has a much better chance of survival. Nevertheless traditional media players with a well-established reputation, recruitment experience and financial backing are finding it easier now to make the move online and are increasingly doing so. Estimates suggest that there are more than 300 job sites of various kinds on the web in Britain, but some of the first firms to launch, such as _www.peoplebank.com_, _www.jobsite.co.uk_, _www. monster.co.uk_ and _www.topjobs.co.uk_, remain market dominators. Some of these claim as many as 500 000 visitors a month, and their combined potential market could be more than 2 million jobhunters, although, of course, many users log on to several sites rather than always going to the same one.

The first companies to have the idea, say, of holding a huge database of people's CVs or job vacancies inevitably got a march on the others and have had more opportunity to develop the technology to stay ahead of the game. It's significant, too, that some of the top sites are associated with big-name recruitment firms. Smaller recruitment firms can now purchase a package that enables them to set up a standardised 'job board' on the

13 How can I protect my personal details? **pages 75, 86.**
14 Am I leaving myself open to computer viruses? **page 86.**
15 How can I stop the spam? **page 88, page 144.**

net, but they will be confined to the way its provider has set it up, and five years on from the pioneer days, it's advertising spend that counts as much as anything in the survival stakes.

This does not mean that big is always best: many small sites offering niche expertise may well provide exactly what you are looking for.[16] But longevity (inasmuch as five years is long-lived) counts highly in the online world.

As for the second principle, it's in everyone's interests for the range of possibilities to expand. A few years ago we might well have assumed that just because sending your credit card details across the internet was possible, it was not necessarily the sort of thing you'd want to do. But although people still voice fears about internet credit transactions as if they were somehow more dangerous than picking up the phone and giving your details to a stranger, it has nevertheless become a standard alternative way of buying things.

Whenever science develops a new technology – take cloning, for example – we know that whatever the moral issues involved, there will be cloned eggs for breakfast tomorrow. The amazing abstract power of the internet is that we can think of things that will make our lives easier, and generally, eventually, someone will find a way of achieving them. Sure, you can't walk your dog on the internet, but you can certainly meet someone who'll do it for you – have a look at *www.dogwalking.co.uk* if you don't believe it.

Few people actually like looking for a new job, however much they might be desperate to get one. While public perceptions of the internet may still often be that it exists purely to give people more opportunities to make money from selling us things, particularly embarrassing things such as pornography, its real *raison d'être* is to make things in general more convenient. That includes selling things for people who sell them, but it also includes buying things, finding things out, learning things, *achieving* things.

The internet offers these facilities to everyone, too: you don't have to be a computer expert, or a recent graduate who has grown up with e-mail and forgotten how to write longhand. The electronic playing field is a level one. If you're returning to work after a period of unemployment, illness or childrearing, for example, it represent an excellent way to immerse yourself once more in the world of work – and to show your skills are up to date. With the oldest section of the population growing at the fastest rate, the internet also offers new opportunities for people trapped into early retirement: a chance to share skills with younger people, and to develop new ones to enable people to continue working.

16 Where can I find them? **pages 61–63.**

And because the facilities available to you online, whoever you are, really are growing all the time and getting better, it's not just something that you *can* use but something you *must* use if you really want to expose yourself to the maximum number of new opportunities.

> **"Where the jobs are is where the jobhunter needs to be. And as time goes on, more and more jobhunters will just have to use the web if they want to get to all the vacancies. "**
>
> Ben Giddings, content and product manager, Monster.co.uk

What's actually **out there**

OK, so you've had the sales pitch. Once you've accepted that the internet is incredibly powerful, and that anything you might want to be able to do with such a medium you can – if not now, then soon – it's time to take on board the fact that it's not just powerful but easy – and getting easier.

The truly helpful job-related internet sites, for example, are moving towards creating one-stop-shop career centres where you can develop your skills,[17] create your CV[18] and look for jobs[19] all on one site rather than surfing around all over the place. It's in their interests to keep you on board, of course, and it's in yours to have people dedicated to providing all these facilities at your convenience.

Jeff Taylor, founder and chief executive officer (CEO) of Monster.com, the US-based parent of Monster.co.uk, has famously dreamed of websites providing a complete career management service throughout your career, 'from intern to CEO'. In other words, you could register when you're about to graduate, and the site could be your friendly careers adviser and jobfinder until you're sitting in Mr Taylor's own chair. And why not?

Again, this isn't the only way of doing things, and in your passionate quest to be Europe's leading marsupial podiatrist, for example, you might find that such sites have less to offer. The important thing is to be aware of the diversity of what's out there, and make it work for you rather than getting bogged down by information overload.[20]

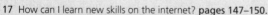

17 How can I learn new skills on the internet? **pages 147–150.**
18 What's the best way to set up a CV? **page 40.**
19 How do I actually search for specific jobs? **pages 36–37.**
20 Any advice on avoiding this? **pages 142–147.**

Let's go into a little more detail, though, and look at how a large jobsite works and how you might engage with it. Popular sites such as Monster, GoJobsite and Stepstone tend to use this model, which has proven itself with jobseekers and employers over time.

The first and most obvious feature that you should come across on the home page is a job search facility. If you want a job, you want to be able to look for one, which is done through a form enabling you to look for current opportunities, often by location (including Europe and further afield, perhaps[21]), job category and keywords.[22] Keywords? These can relate to anything that the employer offering a vacancy has chosen to put in their listings – you'll find much more information about this in Chapter 3. The programs lurking behind all this will then trawl through the database of jobs and display the results for your leisurely contemplation.

Next, there is likely to be a section for your own information – 'My Monster' or 'My GoJobsite', for example. It's this section that makes the site part of your armoury of job-hunting weapons, and it's what saves you from entering the same information over and over again. If you're merely interested in a casual, one-off jobsearch out of curiosity, you can use the search facility outlined above. But if you want to take the whole business more seriously, here you can set up your career profile: in other words, who you are and what you're looking for. Again, there's a more detailed account later in this book; in brief, though, you can use this section to enter your CV into an online database where potential employers can find it, and you can automate and refine the search you tried earlier so that information comes to you rather than you having to go out and look for it.

A third typical section is something on the lines of a 'Career Centre'. This is essentially an information resource,[23] but like the best of anything on the internet it's a two-way medium: as well as simply reading prepared advice on different aspects of jobhunting or particular industries, you can also communicate directly,[24] both with fellow jobhunters who might have useful experiences you can share, and with experts on the other side of the desk.

In addition to these advice resources, you can usually connect to pages of information profiling the companies whose vacancies are listed in the main jobs database. You might already have heard good things from other people about a particular firm and want to

21 How do I find a job abroad using the net? **page 64.**
22 What keywords should I actually use? **page 37.**
23 Where else can I find general information? **Chapters 2, 4, 5.**
24 How can I find real people to ask for advice? **page 63, page 89.**

see if the way it presents itself corroborates that, or you might just want to get a feel of who operates in what sector.[25]

These four sections could be said to form the backbone of most jobsites on the internet, though if you look at the better sites more closely, there will be other facilities to create the sense of a site being a community:[26] everything here is about the business of finding a new job, and information and inspiration can often be found in the margins as much as in the main action.

To recap and step away a little from specific sites, the features related to jobhunting that you can expect to find on major jobsites are:

- searching for job vacancies that might interest you;
- creating an online CV for employers to browse;
- reading articles on different kinds of jobs and how to apply for them;
- researching companies;
- getting answers to your questions;
- sharing experiences with fellow jobhunters.

Inevitably, different sites offer these possibilities in different ways and combinations, but if you're looking at a site that makes grand claims, you could reasonably doubt them if most of these facilities are unavailable. There'll be more detail later about how to tell a good site from a bad one – after all, however clever a search facility is, if it has only a few jobs in the database to start with it can't possibly offer you much.[27]

_____ New routes to **the perfect job** _____

The functions we've just considered are all fundamental to jobhunting on the internet, but if you look back to the list at the very beginning of this chapter, you'll see a lot more besides.

E-mail, for example, is easily taken for granted, and hardly needs to be sold in terms of its convenience as a means of communication. But what, for example, are the legal implications of a salary offer by e-mail?[28] What's the best format in which to send your

---

25 How do I find a firm's website? **page 25.**
26 What other kinds of internet community are there? **Chapter 5.**
27 How can I tell which sites are best? **page 24, page 30, pages 58–59.**
28 What are the legal implications of a salary offer by e-mail? **pages 134–135.**

CV as an attachment?[29] If you write a covering letter by e-mail, do you need to go through the old formal drill of faithfullys and sincerelys?[30] All these questions will be considered in the course of this book, and if you want the answers now, that's fine: just follow the 'hyperlinks'.

Expanding the uses of e-mail, should you sign up to mailing lists?[31] If a career site offers a weekly newsletter, are you really going to read it, or will it end up in your waste-basket every week after an initial month of enthusiasm? Sometimes mailing lists can really offer an insider's insight into a particular area of employment, or even a particular company. How do you get in – and how do you get out?

Mailing lists, like many other aspects of the net, also demand a particular politesse – netiquette, as it's called.[32] The same is true of chatrooms and bulletin boards, and particularly of newsgroups. If you put your cyberfoot in it, you risk being inundated with abusive responses. If you play it cool, however, you can find out just what you want to know.

Technology is developing all the time, and there are forever new formats for data appearing, and new ways for that data to reach you, the user.[33] If you come across an information file or an application form as a PDF, or RTF, for example, what can you do with it? Websites don't always realise that TLAs mean SFA to people.

Now, too, the internet is being repackaged for completely different forms of presentation: on your mobile WAP telephone,[34] for instance, or on TV.[35] The mass coverage of these media is ultimately much greater (at present, at least) than the computer-focused internet as we know it, and employers and recruitment agencies will inevitably exploit their marketing potential to the full. Are you ready to exploit them right back?

Jobhunting is more than simply looking for vacancies or even finding out about the type of jobs you can do: it's also about finding out about yourself.[36] If you're bold enough to wade right into the interactive milieus on offer, people might give you all kinds of advice – some of it good, some of it bad, some of it challenging at least. And the internet

---

29 How should I send my CV? **pages 103–105.**
30 Is it OK to send a covering letter by e-mail? **pages 96–98, 101, 108.**
31 How can I stop being swamped by mailing list messages? **page 83, page 142.**
32 Why can't I just say what I want? **pages 82, 89.**
33 What do all these Three-Letter Acronyms mean? **page 104.**
34 Can I look for jobs with a mobile phone? **page 67–68.**
35 I've got the net on my TV now. What are the implications? **page 69.**
36 How can I learn on the internet? **pages 147–150.**

also offers many opportunities to enhance and practise your skills,[37] as well as assess your suitability for particular kinds of work. All will be revealed.

The important thing is to stay open-minded, and consider new ways of doing things. These new ways can be very rewarding, and ultimately your familiarity with them will make you even more employable.

> **❝Internet recruitment is not really very different. You still have to prove to a potential employer that you have the right mix of skills and experience for the position being applied for.❞**
>
> Sue Hodgson, independent career consultant and former head of university careers service

What's in it **for them?**

One thing you might be wondering with all these promises of convenience, advice and advancement for free is how it can be commercially viable for the people who provide them. Is there a catch?

For the successful jobsites, there is serious revenue in both advertising other services and featuring individual job vacancies and the companies which offer them. A standard arrangement is for a listings fee, either monthly or to display so many vacancies, plus an extra charge to display a company profile, although there are many variations on this model.

It's plainly in everyone's interests for the system to work: more vacancies mean more jobhunters, which in turn encourages more employers to recruit in this fashion – it's a 'velvet circle', with you in the comfiest chair.

Employers make money, or lose less of it, by recruiting effectively and efficiently. Some companies have already found that recruiting via the internet has halved the time it takes to fill a vacancy, and that has a direct corollary for efficiency. Applications are often much better informed as applicants have managed to do a bit of research into the company and the position via the internet, assuming the applicant is suitable, that is. That's a big issue in this field, and at the moment some employers complain as much about receiving details of ill-suited candidates as the jobhunters themselves do about being offered jobs they don't want. We can't entirely stop these things happening, but we can all work to iron them out, and that's why everyone needs to take the system

---

37 Where can I do a real skills profile test? **pages 114–115.**

seriously. The more carefully you follow the advice in this book, the more warmly disposed towards internet recruiting you'll be.

Technology will help, too: online assessment tools are becoming more sophisticated,[38] and in time employers will be better able to filter the candidates as much as you can filter the opportunities. That's if they use the better sites, of course.

The convenience of recruiting through the internet makes the process even more efficient for companies by reducing the time they spend going through applications. Traditionally one way of doing this has been to use agencies – and agencies still have their place, which is important for you as the jobseeker to bear in mind. But agencies can cost the hirer a lot of money, and in some cases they will not have the necessary expertise to know which candidate is suitable for the actual job. Agencies are good at weeding out inappropriate candidates, but not necessarily so good at pinpointing the best ones.

Online recruitment is also directly cost-effective: vacancies are available for searching all day, every day, and in theory there's no limit to the amount of information hirers can post. One Society for Human Resources survey showed that the cost-per-hire on the internet averaged around 90 per cent cheaper than advertising in one of the big newspapers. From the jobhunter's point of view, it generally takes a lot longer to search a newspaper; from the employer's, the web is instant publishing: within minutes of deciding to advertise, the vacancy can be found. Newspaper lead times simply cannot compete, and all this waiting might result in having the vacancy appear in only one edition of the paper. That is not by any means a thorough exposure.

> **"Currently more than 75 per cent of the CVs we screen come from the internet, and more than half of our new recruits come through contact initiated online."**
>
> Mark Whitehead, eLab

According to Forrester Research, at the time of writing corporate recruiters look set to increase their spending on online recruitment by around 50 per cent and cut their spending on newspapers and agencies by around 30 per cent at the same time. It's really happening.

At this stage, of course, newspapers can reach millions of people whereas websites that are reaching hundreds of thousands in the same way are relatively rare. But that's

38 How do I approach an online psychometric test? **pages 115–119.**

changing, and when you consider how many of those millions are actually buying the paper specifically to look for a job rather than just read the news, the internet begins to have an advantage even there. We're not saying give up on the greasy spoon, but at least broaden your diet.

_____ So where **do I start?** _____

The message of this book can be expressed simply:

- ☞ you can use the internet to find a new job;
- ☞ you will be missing out on valuable opportunities if you don't;
- ☞ every aspect of researching, looking for and getting a new job can be done on the internet;
- ☞ the internet is not the only place to try – use it to supplement other methods;
- ☞ above all, try it – and trust it.

When computers first came into the home at the beginning of the 1980s, instruction manuals almost always laboured the point that there was nothing you could type into your computer that would do it any real harm. Power cuts, coffee spillages and small children with plastic bricks were another matter, but the general message was: be brave.

Now that computers are very much part of everyday life, alas the same is not quite true: one ill-judged file deletion can wreck your PC for days on end. Nobody is going to tell you that the internet is completely safe, either: stories in the news of viruses, credit fraud and pornographic bombardment soon put paid to that.

Having said that, it is most unlikely that anything you can type into your e-mail program or web browser will do your computer – or you – any harm, and if you observe certain general cautions, you will find you reap many more golden harvests than thistles.[39] If you want a job, there's no serious harm in using the internet to find it. You can then visit the greasy spoon to read the rest of the news in the spare time you've gained.

Most chapters in this book contain a few suggested exercises at the end. As with every book that has such things, you'll probably feel tempted to read them, nod and then ignore them. But the internet is essentially an active medium, and the more you get

39 Am I at risk from hackers and viruses? **page 86.**

involved with it, the more you find returned to your benefit. Nobody's suggesting you become a bleary-eyed obsessive, sweating at 4am to look for just one more job opportunity. It doesn't need to be like that. But with a little groundwork and openness to new experience, you can make it your servant and not your master. The exercises in this book have just that aim in mind.

Reading every page of this book will probably impart the same knowledge to you that you would gain from trying everything out, but much as we want you to read this, we'd still rather you hit the net – we're encouraging you to gain skills that are best developed in the field. So give it a go.

Final **thoughts**

Maybe you've already heard about people using the internet for jobhunting but thought to yourself: 'But isn't it all IT? If I wanted a job in computers, then sure I'd use the net, it's the obvious place to go, but I want to be a teacher. Teachers don't have either the time to use the net or the resources out there for them to look at.'

Nobody has the time to use the internet all day long apart from internet analysts. And even they probably have enough meetings and paperwork to prevent them from doing that. Home users don't have the money either, of course, to spend every evening surfing, or the inclination to be irradiated by their VDU.

But over the past two or three years, the internet has become vastly more efficient and quick to use, however much a glut of information there might be out there. Bottom-end modems alone have quadrupled in speed in that time, and unmetered access is at last with us in some form. The people who put things on the internet want other people to see them, and even governments have to bow to the sheer force of demand.

The British Government has launched the 'Learning and Work Bank' (more details at *www.employmentservice.gov.uk*), a portal providing details of job vacancies across the country that previously you would have had to find at a Job Centre.[40] It also aims to offer career pages with generic profiles of different types of jobs. 'All anyone will have to do is log on to the site,' said Education and Employment Secretary David Blunkett at its launch. 'A search engine will match the job, careers and learning interests of the individual, helping them transform their lives.' Yes, that's right – on the internet, you can

---

40 What's a portal? **pages 57 and 67.**

have more lives than one, like a cat. And if even politicians have woken up to it, you can be sure it's already happening.

A teacher? An engineer? A secretary? A marine biologist? A doctor? A journalist? A care worker? A financial adviser? A graphic designer? There is information on the internet for all these people, and for everyone else.[41] Think of it as living in a capital city: every interest is catered for somewhere. And if you express an interest in something, fellow enthusiasts will appear out of nowhere.

If you're looking for a job in IT, the internet might well be the first place to look; if you're in a different field altogether, don't make it the last – you'll be missing out.

_____ Your **challenge** _____

Later chapters of this book will explore in detail how best to set up your online CV, for example, and create job search agents. But you can get a long way just by having a go, with a little common sense, and if the results are disappointing, you can turn back to these pages at any time to find out why. So you are invited, right now, to get online and sign up to some of the main jobhunters' sites on the net.

It's assumed for this exercise that you want a new job, and have an idea what field it's in. Don't worry if neither of these assumptions is quite true, there's plenty of time to read the next chapter and refine matters later. For now though, have a go anyway – anything you set up online can be deleted easily enough.

Think of, say, half a dozen jobsites on the net. They don't have to be sites you're directly familiar with: try to think of advertisements you've seen on TV, on the train or on the web itself, maybe when you've visited a search engine or consumer site of some kind, or advertised in a cybercafé. They might be recommendations from a friend or a disaffected colleague. It doesn't matter: just take some time out to look at them, whatever they are.

Go to a search engine, too, and type in whatever you think is relevant, then have a look at two or three of the sites that come up.

Have a go at setting up an online CV on the jobsites – some sites have a link on the home page if it's your first visit. Follow that and let them guide you.

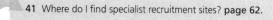

41 Where do I find specialist recruitment sites? **page 62.**

The chances are that if you can spare an hour to throw yourself into all this, you'll learn a lot. You'll also almost certainly find things that are of no interest to you whatsoever. But you'll spot things that are, and get a feel for the way it all works. Now you can surf around the rest of this book, and find out how to make it all *really* work.

CHAPTER TWO

Be a hunter-gatherer

The lowdown on **potential employers**

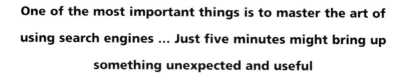

One of the most important things is to master the art of using search engines ... Just five minutes might bring up something unexpected and useful

I n the 1960 film *The Rebel*, Tony Hancock plays a frustrated suburban businessman working in a soulless, dead-end job. He dreams of being an artist. The film begins with him throwing himself into the nine-to-five routine, bowler-hatted like the hundreds of others who catch the same train, with all his creative energy devoted to getting a good seat on it. At work, rows and rows of identically dressed clerks file and stamp and scribble in dull documents – all except Hancock, who idles away his hours producing appalling caricatures of his colleagues in the margins of his ledger books.

'I can't go on ignoring this dynamo throbbing away inside me. Don't you understand? I'm being choked, crushed, bogged down in a sea of triviality. I'm not a machine, I'm flesh, I'm blood,' he cries. 'You can't crush me in a monotous, soul-destroying, everyday routine for ever. Every man must find his own salvation. Live life as it's supposed to be lived ...'

In a sense, of course, none of us 'live life as it's supposed to be lived'. If we did, we'd probably still be hunter-gatherers, dwelling in caves and forests, grubbing for nuts and killing deer whenever we could catch them. Instead, we've chosen to make various contracts to change the way we live. First, to master our environment and stand apart from it rather than be at one with it. Second, to dwell in complex societies, where necessary tasks are divided among people with different tastes and skills. And third, to exchange the use of those skills for money.

Living life as it's supposed to be lived now means fulfilling whatever potential we feel dwells within us. In *The Rebel*, Hancock feels his destiny is to be a great artist, and although the joke of the film is that he has no real talent for it, he nevertheless achieves the fame he's looking for.

In a world where so many things are possible, we all feel that we are entitled to a job that interests, stimulates and even inspires us. And we are educated to expect one – yet so many people feel disaffected and unsettled with what they do. The advantage we have over Hancock's character 40 years ago, however, is a great deal of flexibility. Society and the role of the workplace within it are evolving again, and employers are at last seeing that it is possible for us to use our time in a variety of ways, rather than pouring it all into one. The same person can even be an accountant *and* an artist.

That new flexibility – while it has yet to reach every profession – is itself the very hallmark of the internet.

In the developing workplace, there are many different sectors of work, and many different ways of working within, between and across them. The flexibility of the internet is a great tool in advancing that and pushing or collapsing the boundaries. This can mean many things, including:

☞ teleworking: communicating with your workplace from home as a 'remote unit';[1]

☞ sharing research with people in the same field;[2]

☞ holding meetings in cyberspace (chatrooms, for example);[3]

☞ online training to improve your skills in the job;[4]

☞ gathering leading-edge information.[5]

These are all uses of the internet which are discussed in this book, but if your current concern, like Hancock's, is to get out of a rut, the first way in which the internet is going

1 Are there any resources on the internet for freelancers and teleworkers? **page 66.**
2 How can I tap into professional discussions? **page 83.**
3 How do chatrooms work? **pages 88–89.**
4 How does online training work? **page 149.**
5 What are the best ways to find information? **Chapters 2 and 4.**

to be of serious use to you is as a means of finding out about the opportunities available to you.

One route, particularly if you're certain about the path you want to take, is simply to get hunting for a job straight away using the big jobsites or perhaps a specialist site for your field. If that's the case, then take a look at the following two chapters. But if you're not quite certain of the path to take, or you want to open up your horizons to new possibilities, then what you need is information.

_____ A turn for **the better** _____

What do you want to know? Chances are, you'll find it on the internet. The challenge is knowing *how* to find it and where to turn to.

We've all been in an interview situation and found ourselves being offered the opportunity to ask questions. What do you ask?[6] Often, it's hard to think of anything you want to say. If you already know you don't want the job, then you're only going through the motions anyway. If you think you do want it, you might well decide that your gut feeling is enough.

This chapter isn't going to sit down with you and discuss interview techniques.[7] But if you can be as informed about your subject as possible before you get to the interview – before you even apply for a job in fact – you can be sure that inspiration, and the desire to know just what makes a potential employer tick, is much more likely to strike. You'll benefit from the knowledge, and the employer will be that much more impressed.

It's all too easy in the jobhunting game to become either jaded or complacent: fed up with filling in other people's forms when you've already sent them your CV, or simply unwilling to waste more of your valuable spare time on all this, you just bung a half-page covering letter in the post with a photocopied CV or whack off a quick e-mail then leave it to fate. This is totally understandable, but it's also sending out all the wrong signals.

Where can you turn to make this whole business both more informative and more rewarding? Let's assume that you've decided to find a new job in a particular field. If it's a new area for you, then what you need is to find out, quickly and effectively, just what goes on. If it's already your area of expertise, perhaps you have not really considered using the net to build on the knowledge you already have.

6 What should I ask at interview? **page 128.**
7 *See* **Chapter 8.**

Having decided to embark upon an information-gathering exercise, there are various approaches you can take on the net:

☞ use an internet-based career centre;[8]

☞ contact experts in the field;[9]

☞ trawl the web with a search engine;[10]

☞ look up news and information services.[11]

The large, one-stop-shop jobsites have begun to realise that merely creating epic databases of candidates' CVs and employers' vacancies is not enough – people expect a service. Just as the newspaper job supplements frequently include articles and features on related themes, profiling a particular career for example, or exploring issues such as employment law,[12] so their web counterparts are setting up useful resources of information.

_____ Find **your level** _____

Inevitably, different sites offer different levels of content. A common model is to provide classic tips on:

☞ preparing your CV (online and off-line);[13]

☞ writing covering letters;[14]

☞ interview techniques;[15]

☞ psychometric testing.[16]

8 What do internet career centres offer? Chapter 2.
9 How can I contact an expert? page 74.
10 How do I use a search engine effectively? page 22.
11 Where do I find news and information? pages 20–21, pages 138–140.
12 What are the legal issues for internet jobhunters? page 87.
13 How do I prepare my CV? pages 40–49, page 103.
14 Can I send a covering letter by e-mail? pages 96–102.
15 Can I be interviewed on the internet? page 130.
16 What is psychometric testing? pages 110–113.

Some sites then build on this to discuss various 'issues' such as:

☞ equal opportunities;[17]

☞ working abroad;[18]

☞ salary levels;[19]

☞ education and training.[20]

These are all useful areas to bone up on, but at this stage you want specific information about industry sectors, say, and potential markets for your talents, not the usual generic jobhunting stuff. So look for a section offering, for instance, 'industry advice' or maybe 'communities' where you can find discussions of a particular area.

However, there is one subject under the heading of 'general advice' that you might well find useful at this stage, and that's 'changing careers'. If you've made the decision to go, but you want to leave your whole field as well as the job you're in, this could be the place to start.

_____ The challenge **of change** _____

Remember that the most useful and dynamic sites are always changing. Even if you have combed an entire site, a month later it might well have changed so much that you could do the same again and hardly recognise it. Look out for a 'What's new' button to save you time, or a mailing list newsletter which will let you know when something's changed.[21]

Providing 'content' as it's nebulously called is currently the fashion in cyberspace, but users will soon wise up to being short-changed with dull copy that never varies. Content may be king, but only if it's written by someone wearing a crown. Many jobsites offer a range of articles, but unless they're written by people who really know their subject,

---

17 Is there any information about equal opportunities on the web? **page 152.**
18 How can I find a job abroad using the net? **page 64.**
19 How do I know I'm being offered an appropriate salary? **page 134.**
20 What training resources are there online? **pages 147–150.**
21 Tell me more about newsletters. **pages 83–84.**

don't waste your time reading them. Scroll down the page (if it's not at the top) to find out just whose pearls of wisdom you're collecting. Now and again you'll find an article is actually there to sell the benefits of advertising on that site (for you or for an employer) rather than to offer real information and expert advice. No name? Ask yourself why.

And here's another question to ask yourself: if you can't find the information you're looking for, in some form at least, within a few pages, is this the kind of site you're going to find useful when actually looking for jobs? You can't get something for nothing, even on the internet, but you can expect a certain user-friendliness. If it isn't there, you can go elsewhere.

> **❝At the end of the day good content is down to personalisation, freshness and relevance. The content itself needs to support every career-related decision that the candidate makes and also to help them manage their time outside of the workplace.❞**
>
> Edward Beesley, content manager, GoJobsite.co.uk

—— Let's go **to market** ——

However comprehensive and helpful the big jobsites are, the chances are that they can't tell you everything you want to know. The best you can hope for is to advance your basic knowledge, and then find some leads you can follow up elsewhere.

This suggests another criterion you can use to judge the usefulness of editorial content on a website: whether it offers opportunities to take the matter further. As an analogy, take the online presence of the national newspapers. If a friend mentions that there was an article on growing pomegranates, a subject dear to your heart, in yesterday's *Independent*, you can naturally point your browser to *www.independent.co.uk* and look up the text. What makes it all the more useful is the list of links to related websites or other news stories in the archives that you may be offered. The key with anything on the internet is navigation.

_____ Paper **tigers** _____

Why not try entering a few key words, such as the name of the industry in which you are hoping to find new employment, into one of the national papers' sites? The _Guardian_ (_www.guardian.co.uk_) and the _Daily Telegraph_ (_www. telegraph.co.uk_) in particular offer excellent search facilities. This way you can often find out what the burning issues are, which a generic career centre might not cover.

The same goes for pursuing a line of enquiry about a particular career: a list of further reading to follow up in your local library would be helpful, and a list of web links better still, seeing as the whole point of this exercise is to use the internet.

What kind of links might you find, where will they take you? They might be all manner of things:

- trade organisations
- support groups
- mailing lists[22]
- online newsletters
- newspaper or magazine articles
- company profiles.[23]

Always 'ask around' the subject.[24] Does your chosen field have a union, for example? If so, it will probably have a website. If you haven't come across a link to it at the end of something you've been reading, check out _www.tuc.org.uk_, the Trades Union Congress site, which has information about more than 70 unions and trade bodies. Want to be a dietician? Did you know there's a British Dietetics Association? You can get there (_www.bda.uk.com_) through a link from the TUC site.

22 What is a mailing list? **pages 83–84.**
23 How do I find more about a particular company? **page 24, page 61.**
24 How do I find other resources on the net, such as forums and mailing lists? **Chapter 5.**

If you want to be a farmer, the obvious place to go to is *Farmer's Weekly* magazine. The same logic applies to the internet, and if you know of a publication dedicated to your area, even if it's not one that's available on the newsstands, there's a strong chance that it has a website that might be helpful. Many publications archive all their articles or have extracts on their sites; at the very least you should be able to find some more leads to follow. On that theme, look out for pages of links again.

If you're not sure whether there is a trade magazine for you, then the internet becomes the obvious place to find that out, too. Yahoo! has a categorised directory of trade magazine websites at *http://uk.dir.yahoo.com/Business_and_Economy/Magazines/ Trade_Magazines* and you can also find newsstand magazines at *www.britishmagazines.com* or *www.magsuk.com*. For a more global view, you can track down more than 150 000 publications of all kinds at *www.publist.com*.

One of the most important things is to master the art of using search engines. But even if it throws up huge numbers of irrelevant sites, you should still try typing simply the name of your sector, for example, into one of the top ones and see what comes up. Just five minutes might bring up something unexpected and useful and give you new ideas to ponder or links to follow.

_____ The good **search guide** _____

Most people use search engines, but few know how to use them well. A common complaint is that they offer endless lists of sites with no relevant connection to your enquiry; this is then used as a basis for complaining about the formlessness of the internet in general. Information management is a growing science, however, and if you master a few basic rules, it will make all the difference, although you can't avoid irrelevance to some degree, of course: computers can't think for themselves.

Most of the popular search engines allow you to refine your search criteria in various ways, often using terms such as AND and OR from Boolean algebra, plus and minus signs, and quotation marks. Different engines use different combinations of these, so check the site's instructions. The basic principles work like this:

☞ broaden your search: look for **cats OR dogs**;

☞ narrow your search: **cats -dogs** (ignores any site that refers to dogs; **cats NOT dogs** would do the same on some sites) or **cats AND dogs** (this demands both);

☞ read the small print: on some sites, **cats dogs** looks for either term or both; others (such as Google) insist on both to return a result;

☞ hunt for a phrase: **'raining cats and dogs'** will only return sites with the whole phrase in quote marks;

☞ combine them all: **weather 'raining cats and dogs' -fish** will look for any site that uses the phrase 'raining cats and dogs' and discusses the weather, unless Michael Fish is mentioned (or other fish, for that matter – note that search engines are not usually case sensitive);

☞ think of alternatives: **'cats, persian' OR 'persian cats'**, for example;

☞ if you want to be even more picky, look for an 'advanced search' button;

☞ narrow down the country: add **uk** or **.co.uk** to your criteria, for instance.

Remember: no search engine looks at the whole internet; that simply isn't possible at the moment. What they all do is search their own databases of sites, which are usually updated constantly although they can never keep up with the whole net. The search engines work in different ways, too:

☞ by storing a many-branched tree of categories, e.g. *www.yahoo.com*;

☞ by analysing the way sites link to each other, e.g. *www.google.com*;

☞ by 'reading' as many sites as possible: e.g. *www.altavista.com*.

You can even search several engines at once by using a meta-search facility, e.g. *www.metacrawler.com* or *www.copernic.com*, or ask specific questions: *www.ask.com* (also known as Ask Jeeves).

A warning: some sites, usually the directory-based ones in particular, charge for sites to be listed early on in the results, meaning that you are by no means getting 'objective' data.

_____ Viewed **in profile** _____

It's quite likely that the time will come when you've gathered the names of a few companies that you'd actually like to work for. Why not use the web to find out what they do? There are two main places to look:

 on a jobsite where you know the company advertises vacancies;

 on the company's own website.

In the first case, as you've probably discovered already, most of the jobsites provide 'company profiles' where featured employers can tell you, the punter, a little bit more about their corporate culture and the kind of vacancies that come up. This model is also common among the more specialist sites. While it's a useful way to get a quick summary of what an employer is all about, you have to remember of course that this is also (a) a marketing tool and (b) often a paid-for service. In other words, the company is inevitably going to show its best side, and it may well be paying the jobsite for the privilege, which shouldn't make much difference to you, but it does mean that not all relevant firms, particularly the smaller ones, are necessarily going to be featured.

This first point – that they are out to sell themselves – is inevitable, true of the company's own website (if it has one), too. But at least they are likely to have more space to explain themselves and for you to garner information.

Judging the value of what a company tells you or, more subtly, whether it really can offer an appetising working environment is not something you can do in five minutes, but there are tools to help. The Employer Value Proposition (EVP), for example, is a benchmark system designed to rate 'company culture' from the point of view of people working or wanting to work in it.

Take a look at *www.justpeople.com*. The site presents EVP data as part of its company profiles, showing brief assessments of firms' quality of working environment (based on hours, flexibility, teamwork, etc), pay deals, brand performance and training/promotion opportunities. These are all things you'd probably want to explore further on a milkround open day or at interview, but these charts could help to narrow down your options.[25]

Coming back to content, Justpeople was founded by a former BBC journalist and a former head of global recruitment and has a team of journalists behind it. A good tip for

---

25 What should you do at an interview? **pages 124–125.**

finding a website's credentials is to look for the 'About us' pages, which sometimes reveal the parent company, mission statement and experience of the jobsite's staff. And sometimes they don't …

_____ Firm **findings** _____

It's not usually that hard to find a company's website, as it's in their best interests to be easily available. Try the following:

☞ just type the company name into your browser;

☞ type the name into *www.google.com* and hit 'I feel lucky';

☞ type the company name plus **.co.uk** or **.com**;

☞ if the name is more than one word long, try (a) no space between words, (b) a hyphen between words, (c) an underscore between words: **boggswidgets, boggs-widgets, boggs_widgets**;

☞ if it's an internet or computer-related firm, try adding **.net**;

☞ if it's a government body or department, add **.gov.uk**;

☞ if it's a trade organisation or other body, try **.org** or **.org.uk**.

These days you don't even need to type **http://** or often even **www.** Your browser will work this part out for itself. (Note that some addresses don't begin with **www** anyway: in this book they are always prefaced by http:// to make it clear.)

There are many different levels of site and quality.[26] Don't be put off by sites that are boring, however: sometimes the dullest sites are the quickest to load, and that might just mean you get straight to what you're trying to find out. With the internet, it is often important to tailor your expectations to your needs.

If you're looking for a powerful jobsite database, you will want it to be well designed and offering a high level of functionality, but if you just want a lowdown on, say, how many people work for a company and where its main offices are, bog-standard

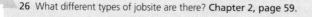

26 What different types of jobsite are there? **Chapter 2, page 59.**

'brochureware' might be as good as or better than a site vaunting trendy special effects.[27] Of course, if you're looking to be a web designer, you might reasonably expect a site to impress you with its design first and foremost, and any content may well be of secondary importance to you.

If your chosen company doesn't have a website, this should not be a reason to condemn it (unless it is involved with the media or the internet itself) – many firms simply don't need to market themselves in this way, or may not have the resources. Having said that, some of them merely *think* that they don't need to. A survey by Best Research at the beginning of 2000, for example, found that not one of the top FTSE 100 companies was using the net to its full potential. They ought to wake up and smell the coffee – you the jobhunter are there, rapping on the glass screen of your monitor.

If you can't find anything about a particular company by looking on the jobsites and it doesn't have its own site, that doesn't mean you can't find anything about it on the internet. Here are some avenues to try:

- type the name into a search engine (*see* The good search guide on pages 22–23): this might reveal references to the company in question on other sites;

- if nothing comes up, try a couple of different search engines, preferably of varying types: they all have their own databases;

- type the name into the search facility on one of the national newspapers' sites: if it's been in the news, you're sure to find it;

- find a relevant trade body and see if someone there can tell you whether your quarry is a member;[28]

- companies that don't have websites often do have e-mail: use the tips in the panel opposite, and get in touch.

27 Tell me more about brochureware, **page 57.**
28 Where can I do that? **page 21.**

———— We know **where you are** ————

Finding someone's e-mail address is not always as easy as general searching for information, but there are various avenues to try:

- ☞ find out the web address of the company, then try various combinations of the person's name like this: *fbloggs@widgetcorp.co.uk*, *f_bloggs@widget corp.co.uk*, *f.bloggs@widgetcorp.co.uk*, *fredbloggs@widgetcorp.co.uk*, *fred.bloggs@widgetcorp.co.uk*, etc;

- ☞ if it's a small firm: *fred@widgetcorp.co.uk*;

- ☞ try phoning up or e-mailing a generic address such as *info@widgetcorp.co.uk* or *contact@widgetcorp.co.uk*;

- ☞ look them up at *www.whowhere.com* or *www.bigfoot.com*;

- ☞ type their name (**'fred bloggs'** or perhaps **'fred bloggs' AND widgetcorp** to narrow down when it's a common name) into a normal search engine; if they've ever posted to a web forum, for example, their address might appear under their message.[29]

———— Don't forget **the old ways** ————

If you have been hunting down a particular company to no avail, or if you are simply tired of doing everything on a computer screen, there are always more traditional ways of finding things out.[30] Nine times out of ten, maybe more, you can find out what you want on the net, but there's no good reason not to go down to the local library, or to thumb the *Yellow Pages* and phone people up, or read the careers sections of the newspapers. If you don't know where your local library is, look it up at *www.scoot.co.uk* or *www.bt.co.uk/phonenetuk* – the latter is basically the Directory Enquiries database available to you online. As for the papers, go to *www.agencycentral.co.uk* – there's a useful list of when each paper carries different types of job vacancies.

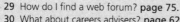

29 How do I find a web forum? **page 75.**
30 What about careers advisers? **page 62, page 118.**

Libraries have long been a very useful resource for the career hunter, and the way they work offers an interesting contrast to the methodology of the internet. If you're already sitting in the library surfing the net, then you've got the best of both worlds. But if you cross the reference room floor to the careers shelves, the first thing you realise is that you can see everything at once in a sense; maybe not the name of every pamphlet or prospectus, but at least the spines of the books on that shelf, and the names of the classifications under which they are filed.

This is something you simply can't do on the internet: when every search engine gives you different results, and with the web itself growing exponentially, you cannot get an at-a-glance feel for everything available to you. What you gain in quantity, perhaps you lose in accessibility.

Having said that, there are definite ways to master the internet and to impose order upon its apparent formlessness – if you learn them now, they will stand you in good stead for the future, and you will be on the road to living life as it's supposed to be lived.

——— Find **yourself** ———

If you want to practise search techniques and finding e-mail addresses, why not look up the company you work for or that of a friend. Then see if you can track down your own e-mail address. Your global profile may not be as low as you thought it was …

CHAPTER THREE

Bring it on

Making the web **work for you**

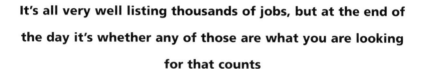

It's all very well listing thousands of jobs, but at the end of the day it's whether any of those are what you are looking for that counts

t's probably just as well that evolution is a long, slow and extremely drawn-out process. Imagine if organisms mutated far more often, and the most adapted to their environment became more dominant more quickly. The ways things are going, the human race would soon stop walking, and even talking – we'd become a race of couch potatoes. And the use of internet recruitment would perhaps accelerate this process as much as anything.

Think of the traditional job searching process: it's not just sitting in that greasy spoon with the newspaper, it often involves a lot of legwork. Visiting agencies all over the place, maybe visiting employers to garner the same information that you now know your mouse can whisper to you. Walking miles simply going back and forth to the post-box.

Once you've learned to find your way around cyberspace, as with everything else in life, the natural move is to look for shortcuts. There are plenty of them out there for the jobhunter in particular, and this chapter will show you where to find them – with the time you've saved, you could go for a nice healthy walk in the country.

One of the all-out best things with the internet is how you can let things come to you rather than constantly having to solicit the information and the opportunities you're looking for. This is very much the way things are developing: the technology is already powerful enough to make the jobs come to you for a change. While no employer is going to want to encourage you to be lazy, it's nevertheless in their interests as much as yours to speed up the recruitment process, and this is one way of doing it.

_____ Looking at **the figures** _____

The whole premise of most major jobsites on the internet, as you've probably discovered already, is that they offer a database of current vacancies which you can search by:

- ☞ category
- ☞ keyword
- ☞ employer
- ☞ location
- ☞ salary
- ☞ level.

Not all sites offer the same search mechanisms by any means, and few offer all of the above. That doesn't matter – it's how you use the facilities that is most important.

Being able to search the listings is all very well, but if you don't find what you're looking for, it can be frustrating. There may be a number of reasons for this:

- ☞ limited number of opportunities listed;
- ☞ your particular type of job is not featured;
- ☞ your search criteria are too broad or too narrow.

In general, the more opportunities you are exposed to the better, of course. A number of the bigger sites in the UK already have more than 10 000 job vacancies on their books, and in general the figures are rising. Every time you go to a site, the vacancies will have changed – and if the numbers have gone down for any reason, you might well ask yourself why. If a site doesn't publish the size of its database somewhere obvious, usually on the home page, that is a good reason to be suspicious.

As ever, though, numbers can be misleading. In some cases, the number of jobs on offer that you see is not limited to the UK but might include partner sites overseas.[1] If the astonishing 123 000 vacancies available include those in the States, the figure might not mean very much to you as a UK jobseeker. PlanetRecruit, for example, advertises itself specifically as an *international* jobsite, and the number of vacancies shown on the home page reflects that.

The number of vacancies is not the only statistic that might be useful to you – or, inevitably, the only one that might be misleading. Treat all data with circumspection, and remember that it's results that count. Having said that, it's also worth bearing in mind:

☞ the number of visitors or hits;

☞ the number of companies featured;

☞ the number of CVs stored.

The first and last of these give an indication of how many people like yourself are actually using the site in question. Monthly visitors/hits is a statistic not often displayed, though, and is an inherently confusing term. 'Hits' in the web world can mean many things, including:

☞ number of different people using the site;

☞ number of times each page has been accessed;

☞ number of times the overall site has been accessed.

It's a minefield, so maybe you should focus more on the number of CVs listed. That figure is probably there to impress potential employers, but it also reveals how many people have found the site worth spending enough time with to go as far as creating a CV on it. Some of those will inevitably have gone stale long ago, but it's still a good indication of the site's quality. What's going to reassure you is some sign that other people like yourself are bothering with this site.

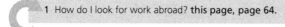

1 How do I look for work abroad? **this page, page 64.**

"Generally I found the experience of jobhunting on the web a useful one – I prefer to look at the jobs onscreen rather than looking through a newspaper. When you find one you want to apply for, it's very easy to save it – and you don't end up with piles of paper lying about. Basically it's just an alternative way of going about something."

Helen Bright, internet jobhunter (and cartographer turned web designer)

Number of companies is also a useful piece of information (although again, not often displayed): if all the vacancies are coming from a handful of major firms, then the market is not truly being represented. The greater the diversity of employers using the site, the wider the variety of jobs on offer. There's no reason why you shouldn't e-mail the jobsite in question and ask for this sort of information.

As ever, there's a caveat: 'employers' in internet recruitment terms can often include agencies. There are many recruitment consultants that use jobsites to post up the vacancies on their books. For you as a committed jobseeker, this needn't be a problem, as it's jobs you're looking for, but don't be surprised if you come across a lot of agencies rather than being led directly to the heart of a particular firm when you click on a link to find more details about a job.

It's all very well listing thousands of jobs, but at the end of the day it's whether any of those are what you are looking for that counts. It's difficult to assess the value of a particular site in this respect, especially given that the listings change from day to day; the only way to get a feel is to give it a go and try a site on a few occasions over a period of time before you decide what you really think about it.

But visiting a dozen websites over and over again is where things really start to become a bore. You need to get on with your life, and you can't spend all day every day trawling through huge databases. After all, the internet is supposed to be making this whole business more convenient – otherwise you might just as well not bother with it. And another thing: if you're doing this at home, you don't want an epic phone bill; if you're at work, you don't want to get sacked from the job you're trying to leave by spending all your time there trying to leave it.[2]

2 What happens if I get caught looking for another job? **pages 140–141.**

Don't despair. What you need are search *agents*, and plenty of the better sites now offer them.

Cut out **the legwork**

In the infamous *Harry Potter* books, messages are delivered by owls which will track you down wherever you happen to be and drop a letter or parcel into your lap. For anyone disappointed that real life can't be more like that of the wizards created by J. K. Rowling, the good news is that we have e-mail, which can do all this and more.

If you took up the challenge in the first chapter, you may well have already set up various job search agents to do your bidding. Either way, in this chapter you'll find useful advice on how to make them more effective. If you're not sure what they are yet, this section is for you.

Put simply, search agents automate the process of looking through a database so that you only have to do it once. In the same way that you enter search details such as keywords or job type, you set up the same criteria and save them on the website in question as a personal 'agent'. You can then forget about visiting the site every day or whatever, and whenever suitable matches are found, the site will e-mail you to let you know.

There are variations within this model. Some sites, such as *www.topjobs.com*, will only send you an e-mail when a match has come up. Others will contact you on a regular basis – daily or weekly, say – and present the matches in one go.

And the way the matches are presented varies significantly, too. In some cases, fairly full details of each match will be mailed to you; in others, just a one-line summary with a link to follow which will take you straight to the full information on the website in question. Others still may tell you that there have been some matches (perhaps saying how many), but you have to visit the site to find out anything about what they are.

You're after an easy life here, and in an ideal world you would probably want perfect matches, with full details (including contacts for applying) e-mailed to you on the spot. But life isn't as simple as that, even on the internet – and there are reasons for it. It's rare for a site to give away quite that much: however grateful you are to it for finding the jobs you want, you are not actually going to bother returning to the site. All of these jobsites thrive on traffic, and they need you to come back.

The deal is that they should make it worth you coming back – if you find it pure inconvenience to return to them, and they do not bring anything new to the experience, then more fool them. The best sites create a culture where you *want* to go back – for job listings, of course, but also for advice and support throughout all stages of the process. This book is as much about the follow-up stages as those of finding a job.[3]

Once you've accepted that you may well have to go back to the site to see full details of the job you're interested in, you can still demand certain levels of service within that model. For example, e-mails from some sites actually say how many matches have been found in the subject line – Stepstone and PlanetRecruit do this. This gives you some idea – and indeed warning – of what to expect. You'll be amazed: some sites can send you two vacancies on one day, and 72 on the next. If you know that the e-mail you're about to open is enormous, you can then save it for a coffee break.

What's more annoying still is that you often find the same vacancies coming up over and over again. To some extent this is simply because the same employers post them over and over again, and it's next to impossible for the site to filter them, especially if each new posting does something sneaky like change the wording slightly – it's a bit like being spammed by e-mail.[4] Look at the tips panel coming up for some suggestions.

Other issues to consider include the possibility of setting up more than one agent at the same site. We all know that submitting search criteria to forms on the internet is not always entirely satisfying, and you may feel you are being forced into certain keywords that do not entirely cover what you're looking for. If you could just send out another agent, with slightly different details …

Often, you can. At *www.monster.co.uk*, for example, you can save up to five different search agents as part of your personal profile on the site ('My Monster'). PlanetRecruit calls them 'mailouts' and GoJobsite 'search strings'; again, you can save a clutch of them. They can be wildly different from each other or vary in only the smallest detail. If you really want to keep your options open, you could search for astronaut jobs with one and commis chef posts with another.

This technique is a bit like compiling different CVs tailored to different jobs you're hankering after, only much less time-consuming – and you can set up different online CVs in a similar way.[5] You might well be advised to avoid setting up *too* many agents, however, or information overload will set in and you'll never find the real job offers lost in the endless forest of opportunities that your e-mail inbox has become.[6] What you want to do is make a few agents work really effectively.

3 What else do the jobsites offer, apart from jobs? **Chapter 2, page 59.**
4 Spammed – what the hell is that? **page 88.**
5 How do I set up an online CV – or several? **page 40.**
6 Help! How do I cope with all this data coming in? **pages 142–147.**

_____ Weeding out what **you don't want** _____

If you're going to set an agent on the trail of a killer job, you'd rather it were Sherlock Holmes than Inspector Clouseau. You don't want it dragging back any old job like the cat bringing half-eaten birds to your doormat and expecting praise for it.

The quality of the results you get will depend on three things:

☞ the quality of the jobs;

☞ the quality of the agent;

☞ the quality of the way you use it.

There's nothing you can do about the first of these, apart from exercise your judgement in choosing which sites to use.[7] The same applies to the quality of the agent, i.e. the criteria by which you are able to search a particular database or the way in which its mechanisms actually work. Of the possible options listed at the beginning of this chapter, some are obviously more useful than others, and it will depend upon your priorities. If you don't mind where you work, then the location factor obviously loses importance.

The main area of concern for anyone lies with categories and keywords. Categorising a database of jobs by type offers clear benefits, but also disadvantages in that different people sometimes refer to the same job by different titles. To take a media example, most magazines and newspapers employ people known as sub-editors who take the writers' copy and either ruin it or make it readable, according to which side of the fence you fall. The job of a 'sub' can also involve laying out pages and doing design work, but not necessarily. And the titles given to people who undertake these tasks can be any of the following and more: sub-editor, production editor, production assistant, editorial assistant, assistant editor, editor, copy editor, etc. That's not even taking into account the fact that some employers have large teams of such people, with chiefs, deputy chiefs and so on. So if you're looking for a job as a sub, are you sunk from the start?

Well no, as most sites invoke more general categories: you'll probably find these jobs under 'media', for example. 'Media' itself, however, can be lumped with 'marketing', say, or with 'arts'. Every site does it differently, and this is one reason why having the option of saving several agents can be a great benefit to you. The main thing is to be alert, and consider being broader-minded in terms of categories than you think you might need to be.

---

7 What makes a good jobsite? **page 24, page 30, pages 59–60.**

Keywords are more complex still, yet ultimately your most powerful tool. Again, different sites mean different things. In the case of Monster, for example, the agent will search the full text of relevant jobs (i.e. ones that match your other criteria) for the occurrence of whatever words you have chosen. Other sites, however, will predefine keywords for a particular post, and you may be restricted in your choice; or the search will be applied only to the keyword list for a job rather than to the whole text of the job description.

It's actually very similar to the way different search engines work.[8] Some just trawl through the <META> tags of sites on the web (i.e. the keywords put into the code by whoever designed the site), while others look through absolutely everything, and then either pick out keywords for themselves or store the actual text of the site.

Using keywords effectively takes a certain amount of experience, and although the aim here is to make internet jobhunting as painless as possible, you will have to be prepared for a little trial and error at the start to get the feel of things. Sometimes you need to make your search more specific, especially if you're being inundated with dross, and sometimes less so.[9] It won't take long to get the hang of it, though – take a look at the panel to find out exactly what the sites' experts say.

How long can you expect all this to take? Most search agents will start e-mailing you matches, if they have any, within 24 hours; if it takes more than a week, there's definitely call for changing your keywords – or changing the site you use.

The Monster guide
to search agents

What happens if you're getting no results, or far too many? Search agent expert Ben Giddings of Monster.co.uk has the answers.

☞ **Why aren't the matches more precise?**

Agents match jobseeker criteria with client information, and to get a near-perfect match, you need to be exceptionally prescriptive in terms of what information you allow either the employer or the jobseeker to put in. But no recruiter would accept such rigidity, so you have to try to get a balance between a tight

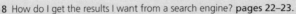

8 How do I get the results I want from a search engine? **pages 22–23.**
9 What happens if I get job details from sites I didn't even sign up to? **page 87.**

search and giving the recruiters all the freedom and flexibility the internet offers them to talk about themselves.

How do I get the best out of my keywords?

My advice is not to be too specific. Better to get too many results than too few. You can use further keywords to refine your search from the results page on Monster. On Monster, our keyword search scans every word of a job advert, which means if you put in the keyword 'manager', your results will include every advert that contains the word 'manager'. So you could get an assistant or trainee position where the job 'reports to the Marketing **Manager**'. Keywords are best used if the user knows that keyword will be specific to the job they are looking for. For example, if you are after an accountancy position but your specific interest is retail, you can do a search on the Accounting/Auditing category using the keyword 'retail'. That should narrow the search to retail-based accountancy positions.

I've done all that, but strange things still happen. Is it me?

Keywords are very good at defining and redefining searches. They are also very good at messing them up. Again it comes back to learning how to get the best out of the functionality. It also relies on recruiters putting useful information in their ads (so the keywords are picked up on searches) and putting their adverts in the right categories (recruiters often post their own jobs).

And if absolutely nothing comes up?

It could mean we don't have any relevant jobs for you. There will always be people who can find more relevant jobs elsewhere, and best of luck to them. It's far better to get a fulfilling career than to use a site that currently doesn't meet your needs.

Quickfire tips for search agents in general:

- refine your search once you've got some initial results;
- use Boolean operators such as AND and OR;
- rule out words you definitely don't want to appear (e.g. use 'NOT sales');
- think how employers phrase things;

☞ set up different agents with different combinations.

A final word from an expert at another of the popular sites, Edward Beesley of GoJobsite.co.uk: 'I would say that if you are entering the search string criteria that you feel are most accurate for you and your career aspirations and you are still receiving positions that are totally wide of the mark, then you need to contact the customer support department of the site you are using.'

Your shop window: **online CVs**

In your challenge to get the jobs to come to you, setting up agents is only one half of the deal. The other is to create an online CV, a term which itself can mean various things. We've already considered the fact that many sites proudly say how many CVs they have listed, but what exactly does that mean?

Essentially there are two poles, with various possibilities in between: at one end, you have a CV formatted and constructed by you, and at the other a situation where you are obliged to tailor your skills and experience into a format entirely determined by the site you're using. As ever, each has its own advantages.

One of the few downsides of the internet in this respect is that it takes away various possibilities in the creation of your CV.[10] For a traditional paper CV, you have the option of choosing the fonts, the colour of paper, and all manner of other fancy options (although you're not recommended to take them). Online, the medium demands a little more consistency. This can work to your advantage: it should be your skills you are selling, not your ability to choose fancy stationery – unless you want to be a stationer.

Let's look at the predetermined end of the spectrum first. Many of the better sites now have sophisticated CV-creation 'wizards' that help you format a complete, professional-looking CV, building an easy-to-use template to fill in online full details of your past, present and hoped-for future. This process can take some time – Monster, for example, warns that half an hour or so is needed. Don't be put off, though: it offers the same advantages as setting up search agents, in that a one-off effort can reap rewards, with you barely lifting a finger to the mouse. Once you have created your online career profile, the effort is all on the part of the employers. They want to fill their vacancies quickly, so they will happily trawl through your details while you're busy doing something else.

10 Are there any other limitations of the internet? **Chapter 10.**

Sending out speculative CVs by post is an infamously laborious – and costly – process. Here, you do it once, and you don't even have to decide which employers to target. They will come to you.

There are ways and means to go about doing all this, and the more carefully you approach it, the better hits you'll get. Make sure from the start that you have thought seriously not just about what you've done before but also about what you really want for the future. A good pro forma online CV will have spaces dedicated to just that.

Observing the **proper form**

Filling in online CVs is generally pretty straightforward, but there are various tricks that can help and things to avoid:

- ☞ to select a block of entries from a drop-down list, use [SHIFT-CLICK] on your PC to select the first and last, and those in between will be selected automatically;

- ☞ to select a few entries in different places, use [CTRL-CLICK] on a PC or [SHIFT-CLICK] on a Mac;

- ☞ press [TAB] on a PC or Mac to jump quickly from one field to the next: it saves your mouse wrist from extra work;

- ☞ if you see options as little circles to click ('radio buttons'), you can select only one option from the list available;

- ☞ with options in the forms of squares with a cross in them when selected ('checkboxes'), you can choose as many as you want;

- ☞ check everything through before you click 'Submit' – there's often a 'Reset' button if you've messed it all up, or you can go *back* through the fields with [ALT] + [TAB];

- ☞ if an error occurs, read the message carefully: sometimes if you click the Back button in your browser, your data will reappear, and you can try submitting it again;

- ☞ if it doesn't reappear, you may have to start again: but check the homepage of this section (e.g. the My Monster page in the case of *www.monster.co.uk*) to make sure your information hasn't been saved after all;

- ☞ don't spend time lining up your details in columns – it won't come out like that at the other end.

It can take time and effort to do a CV, whatever the medium, but you should take it seriously. If you're doing it online, think in particular about what title to give it, as this is what the employers will see first – there's more on this in the online CVs panel below.

The Monster guide
to online CVs

☞ **Think about the type of company that will invest in CV searches**

It's likely to be a large-scale operation with specific (often large-scale or regular) needs in a competitive sector, or a recruiter looking for someone with highly specialised skills. In some cases you're better off going to a niche site.[11]

☞ **Think carefully about the title you give your CV**

A CV title is the first thing an employer sees when presented with a list of potentially suitable CVs and your title has to say a lot about you in only a few words. 'Graphic design' says what field you work in, but the employer should know that already because they've just done a search for graphic designers. What about 'Senior Designer with International Agency', or even 'I did the Guinness ad' – they say much more.

☞ **Don't overdo the attention-grabbing**

On the web, the words you choose to label yourself with count for a lot. Call your CV 'Slartybartfast the wonder Java guru' and no one will give you a second look. Give your CV the title 'Expert Java (3 yrs) & European Project Management' and people get interested. Recruiters want information, not slogans.

☞ **Remember to renew**

Monster.co.uk gets around 1500–2000 new CVs a week posted on to the board. As more CVs are added, yours moves further down the list, making it less likely to be seen by an employer. To combat that, it's probably advisable to 'renew' your CV every month or so. This is normally a feature that you use to post your CV back on the board after one year (at which point it automatically becomes

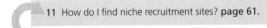

11 How do I find niche recruitment sites? **page 61.**

unsearchable). But if you renew every month or so, each time the database thinks you have posted a new CV and puts it back at the top of the most recent list, thereby keeping you up there with the newest ones. You can renew your CV just by clicking a link on 'My Monster' homepage.

Remember your audience

As well as thinking about what kind of employer is looking through the site you're using, think about the actual information they're looking for, and make sure you include it in the body of your CV. Include any technical aspects of your work – the employer might be looking for something precise such as 'C++'.

Set up more than one CV

Some jobsites will let you create more than one CV, each with its own title, just as you can with some search agents. Think of the different aspects of the work you are looking for, and employers sometimes target people like you in different ways. Put yourself in their field of vision in different ways – and again, remember to renew them all regularly to stay there. For examples, see Figures 1 and 2.

Not every jobsite is terribly sophisticated, and some will simply invite you to upload your present CV as an attachment.[12] Don't have one ready? Read the golden rules on pages 46–49. Most will accept a document in Microsoft Word format, and this does at least give you quite a bit of scope for being 'creative', but don't be tempted to overdo it. Like you, employers are in a hurry, and they too are using the internet for an easier life. Try to give it to them.

Other sites go for some kind of compromise between do-it-yourself and fill-in-a-form, usually employing a looser kind of form into which you can cut and paste various elements of the CV you've already got. This sounds like a helpful way to go, and can certainly save a lot of time, but you still need to think of who's going to be reading it. A little more time to reformat for the web will be to your advantage, although you don't have to go too far, as GoJobsite.co.uk content manager Edward Beesley points out: 'The best advice would be to keep your CV in the standard form and also keep an amended plain text version that can be easily pasted into an online form.'

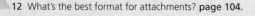

12 What's the best format for attachments? **page 104.**

Chris Test	Daytime Tel: 01234 567890
1 Main Street	Evening Tel: 01234 567890
London AB1 2CD	Mobile: 07234 567890
jon@monster.co.uk	Fax: 01234 567890

Sample CV – Advertising
CV #2998348

OBJECTIVE To obtain a management position at an industry-leading company

TARGET JOB
Desired Job Type: Permanent
Work Load: Full-time
Salary: 30,000 GBP Per Year
Site Location: On-Site

Description of my 'perfect' job:
An opportunity to contribute to the growth of a company

TARGET COMPANY
Company Size: Medium (100–999)
Category: Advertising/Marketing/Public Relations

Description of my ideal company:
A company that empowers its employees, and has an open-door management policy.

TARGET LOCATIONS UK-London UK-NW

WORK STATUS UK I am authorised to work in this country for any employer.

EXPERIENCE 6/1997–Present Advertising Ltd. Anytown, County
Advertising Manager
Manage a team of seven advertising representatives who handle ad placements for a total of 150 clients. Responsibilities include developing media plans and Internet strategies for clients, as well as developing creative platforms, and overall account service. Directly responsible for generating £1m in ad revenue.

2/1996–6/1997 Ads 'r Us PLC Acity, County
Advertising Representative
Responsible for co-ordinating weekly ad placements. Specific duties included: client interaction, media planning, space reservations and billing.

5/1995–2/1996 Ads 'r Us Acity, County
Administrative Assistant
Handled general office duties including data entry, space reservations, answering phones, greeting visitors and billing enquiries.

EDUCATION	12/1998	Central College	UK-London-Atown, County

Secondary school or equivalent
Completed coursework in Advertising Strategies, Direct Marketing, and Branding.

	5/1995	City University	UK-Manchester-Anotherton, County

Bachelors Degree
BA (Hons) Marketing and Communications. Class 2:1

AFFILIATIONS	1/1/96–Present	Advertising Association	Member

SKILLS

Skill Name	Skill Level	Last Used	Experience
Public Speaking	Expert	Currently Used	5 years
Management	Intermediate	Currently Used	4 years
Microsoft Office	Expert	Currently Used	8 years
Spanish Speaking	Intermediate	2 years ago	7 years

REFERENCES

A. N. Other   Ads 'r Us   Advertising Manager
Phone Number: 09876 543210
Reference Type: Professional
W. Normal
Phone Number: 05678 432109
Reference Type: Personal

ADDITIONAL INFORMATION

'Make Yourself Heard' course in Public Speaking – 4-day in-house training, March 1997
References available upon request.

Figure 1 A sample CV

Joe Bloggs
Wardour House
Old Kent Road
London SE1 5ES
UK
jbloggs@provider.co.uk

Daytime Tel: 020 7955 7321
Mobile: 078 41327921

Sample CV – IPD Qualified Human Resources Specialist

CV #75105

OBJECTIVE
IPD qualified graduate with 6 years' generalist HR experience seeks a multinational corporation to utilise HR skills, with a view to progress to senior management level.

TARGET JOB

Desired Job Type:	Permanent
Work Load:	Full-time
Salary:	30,000 GBP Per Year
Site Location:	No Preference

Description of my perfect job:
A position that enables me to use my knowledge of international and general Human Resources skills.

Career Level:	Mid Career
Date of Availability:	From 1 to 3 months

TARGET COMPANY

Company Size:	Large (1000+)
Category:	Telecommunications

Description of my ideal company:
A multinational corporation, with good career development and a forward-looking IT policy with respect to the HR function.

TARGET LOCATIONS

Relocate:	Yes
UK	UK-London UK-SW and Wales

WORK STATUS

UK	I am authorised to work in this country for any employer.

▷

EXPERIENCE

6/1999-Present   CADA plc   London

HR Adviser – International

Working at the head office dealing with international HR. Duties include:

– international employment law advice;
– videoconferencing interviewing for international postings;
– processing international assignees; and
– developing competency matrix for the technical staff.

8/1996–5/1999   Teletel Ltd   London

Human Resources Adviser

I had the responsibility for international staffing in Teletel's EAMS region. Duties included:

– compensation and benefits;
– employment law;
– appraisal and discipline;
– liaising with external recruitment agencies;
– internal advertising campaign;
– processing of international assignees (visas, orientation, travel); and
– MS Access database creation and maintenance.

9/1994–7/1996   First National   Nottinghamshire

HR Team Member

Member of the team that advises line managers and the executive team on issues relating to employment law, recruitment, best practice HR and comp HR initiatives. Duties included:

– graduate recruitment;
– maternity issues;
– personnel planning;
– compensation issues; and
– employee development.

6/1993–8/1993   Midi Ltd   London

HR Internship

Worked as an intern during the summer vacation to gain valuable commerce experience. Skills gained:

– employment law;
– interview strategies/techniques;
– appraisal strategies/techniques;
– staff induction/training.

EDUCATION	6/1994	BSc Honours – Management Studies	UK-London

Bachelor's Degree
Obtained a first-class Honours degree in Management Studies, Major in Human Resource Management.

	6/1990	Tarpoley County High School	UK-Cheshire-Tarpoley

Secondary School or equivalent
A Levels – English Literature (Grade B)
A Levels – Mathematics (Grade B)
A Levels – Human Biology (Grade C)
A Levels – Geography (Grade B)

AFFILIATIONS	10/1998–Present	Institute of Personnel and Development Full Member		

SKILLS	**Skill Name**	**Skill Level**	**Last Used**	**Experience**
	MS Access	Intermediate	Currently Used	4 years
	General Computer	Intermediate	Currently Used	10 years
	Literacy MS Office	Intermediate	Currently Used	6 years
	Public Speaking	Intermediate	Currently Used	5 years

Figure 2 A sample CV

Top tips for **CV writing**

No rules: there are no hard and fast rules, so be yourself. Don't use a template of any kind – what you need to be saying depends on your individual circumstances. CV grammar is unique: try to avoid using first or third person; go for action and process phrases, and solid, quantifiable achievements (e.g. 'innovator in terms of staff training, suggesting and delivering an Investors in People programme that coincided with a 20 per cent reduction in wastage'). There are no sentences in a CV, so turn off the grammar checker and use a style that will feel right to a reader with a decent education.

USP style (unique selling points): make a list of the strongest points you want to communicate before you even start. These might be your knowledge, experience or track record, or they could be a mixture of factors that give you the right profile for an ambitious career change.

Content range: your CV needs to embody those strongest points that apply to you, so you should tailor the style and format to match what you want to communicate. It is possible to create both a chronology of jobs and a skill-based profile in the same CV, but keep your mind mainly on your *unique offering*, which will be a mixture of elements.

Information architecture: do not clutter your CV with trivial detail; your personal details can go at the back on page two. Start your CV with your name, the fastest way to contact you, and a short phrase that sums up your professional role and status (e.g. National Sales Director). Next comes a short introduction (that does not need any heading) to summarise at a glance your main strengths. Do this last, when you are clear what your main strengths are, and incorporate your headline results (which may be figures or may be structural achievements (e.g. 'devised successful new marketing model and planned national roll-out, achieving 10 per cent market penetration within six months').

Skills listing: if qualifications are all important (as for new graduates), lead off with your education. If experience is more important, create a brief section entitled 'Professional' and list your key skills as bullet points. For some people there will be a mix of knowledge and experience that can be easily merged together in this 'Professional' section format. If you are technical, incorporate within that section a brief 'Technical Resume' that summarises not just what you know but what you do with it.

Unextended career: if your work experience is limited, problematic or less than totally relevant to the next job you want, don't try to imitate a major league CV style by listing every trivial skill and experience. Summarise and prioritise. Think around everything you have done (e.g. graduate gap years) and describe it briefly in a way that shows your best character attributes. Remember that potential can sometimes be as important as track record.

Extended career: the presentation of a complex career narrative is not easy; it may take several attempts over a number of days before you slash the dross and distil out the convincing material. Start by writing the whole thing as a story for your own benefit. List the main themes. Then find a layout where you can use bullet points to cover your roles, achievements, progression, contribution, innovation, whatever. Next create the briefest version you possibly can of your present/recent job, adding anything you missed later. Finally, summarise earlier jobs so that you do not repeat yourself – two pages is the max you have.

Test your CV: before you start using your CV in earnest, try it out on friends and associates and ask for critical feedback. Send it to a job you are not desperate about and ask for feedback. Tke time to refine it and don't leave anything until the very last moment.

The online angle: the point about creating a brilliant CV first is that you can post it for applications requiring that method, you can e-mail it as an attachment (Word 97 or higher; universal font such as Tahoma, Veranda, Times or Trebuchet; no graphics) and you can cut and paste from it when filling out an online application or creating an online profile. **Do the CV first; launch it on the internet when you have it right.**

© Steven Holmes and John Peters. This section is licensed for publication by Monster. You can contact them for advice and assistance on *www.cvservices.net*.

All this means is looking carefully at the fields into which the online CV has been divided (if any) and repackaging your details accordingly. Computers like consistency more than anything else and it's best that you try to summarise your previous work, say, in a regular fashion (employer, job title, achievements or responsibilities, whatever is appropriate). Long passages of discursive text are never necessary; quickfire bullet points are always better, online or otherwise.

Another issue worth mentioning is whether you are really serious enough at this stage to send out your trusty CV to the world at large. Edward Beesley warns of a troublesome side effect of setting up too many online CVs: 'If you are not a serious jobhunter, then repeated calls from interested recruitment consultants can get a bit tiresome. So perhaps if you are just *thinking* of putting your CV online you could take off your telephone number and leave your e-mail address, remembering to include your telephone number for any direct applications.'

Finally, there are of course security issues – there are tales of data from one site appearing on another, and if you've registered your details on a wide range of jobsites, don't be surprised if a few others mysteriously start e-mailing you.[13] The simple solution is to read the small print on the sites you use – none of the reputable ones will pass on your details without your say-so. Follow the hyperlink to read more about this important question.

CVs – **the golden rules**

There are certain maxims which apply to any form of your CV:

- who's reading it I: what are they looking for?;
- who's reading it II: they don't have much time – be brief;
- every CV should say (a) who you are (b) what you're doing (c) where you are;
- make sure your current or past job titles actually describe what you do or did, even if your official job title is not quite the same;
- explain your jobs in terms of results – what have you *achieved*?;
- don't include anything you don't really need, and that includes references.[14]

What do they **see in you?**

It has been stressed that you need to think about the end viewer of your CV. So what do they actually see, and how do they find you? The way employers use a site such as *www.monster.co.uk* is very much the same as it is for you, except that they're coming from the other direction. For example, they too can set up search agents. Instead of trawling the vacancies, however, they trawl the CVs. They can enter keywords, too, and these will

---

13 Is my personal data safe? **page 86.**
14 What about references? **page 103.**

search the text that you have entered. This is why it is so important to put some thought into your online CV rather than just bashing it out. It's easy to think that it won't matter if you type in something hastily and then click a few buttons to submit it, but why be so cavalier? You have nothing to lose in creating an online CV, but you can always maximise your gain.

The main difference for the employer is that they are probably paying for the privilege of looking at your CV: they are likely to subscribe to various services provided by the site which enable them not just to look through CVs but also to append notes to them and store them for future reference in something similar to the online 'shopping baskets' you see on sites such as *www.amazon.co.uk*. Your challenge is to catch their eye – and reading the particular site's content on CV building, scanning its help pages and following the tips in this chapter can help you tailor your CV. It also means knowing how to sell yourself in more traditional ways – the golden rules again.

> **"We try to screen all CVs we receive. Given certain skill/experience requirements we'll generally progress with a candidate if their CV radiates a personality compatible with our ethos: energy, enthusiasm and entrepreneurs. "**
>
> Mark Whitehead, eLab

_____ What recruiters **are looking for** _____

Relevance: recruiters are deluged with hopeless applications, attracted by the money but not even addressing the basic job definition. Irrelevant applications never get anywhere. Recruiters are as professional at their job as you are at yours and they spot the wrong-uns within seconds. They do not even read naff-looking CVs containing the wrong information.

Information: your CV needs to be structured to give them the information that *they* are looking for. Usually they tell you what that is in the advertisement or online posting and if you don't understand what they are saying, you probably would not be right for the job.

Convergence: your covering letter and CV can be tweaked to pinpoint your case. Recruiters warm to candidates who show they have thought about the application and where possible have taken the trouble to find out about the job and company.

Corroboration: recruiters are looking for skills that match requirements and evidence of using those skills effectively. Unsubstantiated claims in the US style are hopeless – you need to establish and prove that you are the professional you say you are (e.g. 'good communication skills' makes you squirm but 'renegotiated and then continued ownership of a growing £3m business alliance that was previously failing' shows that you can communicate).

What more: sometimes people respond to expressions of vision and possibility that exceed their stated requirements. For jobs over £45k a year you aren't even starting to compete if you don't suggest that you have fresh ideas to bring to the interview. For big jobs they appoint big candidates who can offer something really positive.

© Steven Holmes and John Peters. This section is licensed for publication by Monster. You can contact them for advice and assistance on *www.cvservices.net*.

_____Home is where **the heart is** _____

One of the key ways the web works is the use of links to take you to further information when you need it. With this in mind, you may well have considered creating a special homepage online for yourself. This too has its own pros and cons.

If you're going to create a homepage for your CV, think about how people will find it. Is it worth your time and effort, and theirs? Do you know how to create one quickly and effectively? Are you looking for work in a market where this sort of skill will impress, or will it just be regarded as a gimmick? Your time is valuable, so use it wisely.

If you've created a CV online on your own web page, there's precious little chance that an employer will simply happen upon it. What it does offer, however, is the opportunity to expand on what you may have already told them elsewhere. For example, the better online CV builders will include the option of a link to your homepage. Unless you're looking for work in the internet industry itself, it's unlikely they will hold it against you if you don't take this option; but if you feel the online CV doesn't offer enough scope to really show them who you are, this could be a useful avenue. Don't overdo it, though: employers are as protective of their time as you are, and unless you've really got something worth demonstrating (and that briefly), you might as well build another CV on a jobsite rather than spend the time going it alone.

The Monster guide
to homepages

☞ Be sure you really need one

Certainly a website can be a good online portfolio for those who are in an appropriate industry (creative, journalism, advertising, etc). And when a studio manager or similar is looking for such people, a website is a very good way of sizing up someone's abilities. However, for non-creative people, there may be little point. You should be able to say everything you need to with your CV.

☞ Does it really represent you well?

You have to ask yourself: is your website such a good, true, professional representation of your skills, talents and personality that you would happily be judged on that and that alone? If the answer is yes, you are probably a highly skilled and experienced web designer.

☞ Keep it simple

Again, unless you're looking for work as a web designer, you should avoid bandwidth-consuming frills. It should be as straightforward as your real CV, but in that case, you have to ask yourself again whether you really need it.

☞ Use the tools

If your homepage is specifically intended to promote yourself, you might as well get it done efficiently. If you have no wider need for HTML skills, for example, you'd be better off using a package such as FrontPage, or even setting up a template-based page through a free web space such as *www.tripod.com* or *www.geocities.com*.

☞ Advertise – but briefly

If you have set up a homepage, you might as well say so in your online CV, but just give the URL rather than anything else. Anyone who's really interested will look for themselves. And give the full address – *http://www.myhomesite.co.uk* or whatever – as some online CV builders will then allow potential employers to go there just by clicking on the name.

How do you know you've had visitors? Everywhere we go on the web, we leave muddy footprints.[15] If you have your own homepage, it's not particularly easy to find out exactly who's dropped by, but it is possible, and it's worth checking with your service provider whether they can offer statistics about visitors to your site – these could show the URLs from which your visitors found you, although that may not actually tell you who they are. Ask the ISP if there's a free site log.

Coming back to your formatted online CV on the jobsites, some of these will actually tell you how many employers have dropped by. Don't expect the jobsites to tell you exactly which employers have read your CV, however: if you've got something to sell and someone peers in your shop window, it's not usual to run outside after them. You would probably be disconcerted if every employer whose vacancy you had read knew you had looked at it – a certain level of privacy is necessary for the system to work.[16]

If you really want to use your time as effectively as possible, automating your job search in the ways explored in this chapter is the way forward. But if you're on a long train journey, there's no reason why you shouldn't read the paper, too. And if you'd rather not rest on your laurels, read on.

---

15 What sort of footprints am I leaving? **pages 86–87.**
16 Can anyone see my data? **page 86.**

_____ Double **your chances** _____

Go to your jobsite of choice and set up two versions of your CV: it'll take a bit of time, but it's worth doing. You can probably use the same model later on for other sites – save everything you've done as plain text in a file on your PC just in case.[17] Now monitor their progress over a couple of weeks. If one CV gets more views from interested employers (the site should tell you how many have looked), ask yourself why. You can then feed this information back into the system to make your main CV better.

_____

17 Tell me more about file formats, **page 104.**

CHAPTER FOUR

Shop around

Making the most of **the new technologies**

The great power of the web, but also one of its disadvantages, lies in the fact that it offers unlimited publishing space

The best military strategists, having sent orders to their troops, do not sit idly by in their clubs sipping port. Rather, they are stooped over the map once more, considering, plotting for the future, and looking for new lines of attack. The same should go for you.

Using search agents and setting up an online CV can successfully form the backbone of your new, internet-age jobhunting strategy, but if you're serious about exploring as many new opportunities as possible, there's no excuse for resting on your laurels. There is still plenty more to discover on the internet that may help you in your quest, which these next two chapters will explore.

> **❝Personally, I think that the value of the internet lies in its diversity and range of information sources and you should be encouraged to explore these as much as possible. I have several favourite websites that I always turn to first and use regularly, but I am always trying others and on the lookout for new ones.❞**
>
> Tom Campbell, futurologist, New Media Knowledge (*www.nmk.co.uk*)

_____ Building **blocks** _____

You'll have seen by now how different kinds of employers have different levels of presence on the internet, but there's a lot of jargon used out there.[1]

The internet is sometimes compared to a large city like London: there's room for everyone there, and no matter how obscure an interest, there's sure to be a website, support group or chatroom out there for fellow obsessives. The city idea offers an analogy for the way the net is constructed, too: just as almost every street in London contains a variety of architecture, with glass skyscrapers jostling for attention with elegant Georgian town houses and dull grey blocks, so the web has its own different styles of architecture. It's worth spending a little more time strolling down its streets to see how it all fits together.

The great power of the web, but also in a sense one of its disadvantages, lies in the fact that it offers unlimited publishing space. Naturally 'space' (which means memory on a computer somewhere) comes at a price, but compared with any other way of presenting information to the world at large, it's a cheap one.

So the term 'website' that we bandy about so glibly covers a lot of things: if you've set up a single page to promote your enthusiasm for terrapins, that's no less a website than the enormity of *www.microsoft.com*, say. What ultimately differentiates sites is the links that are made between them. The number of external links to *www.myterrapins.org.uk* is probably going to be countable on the thumbs of one foot, but who doesn't know where to find Microsoft on the web, even if it's not where they want to go today?

The biggest websites are now running into millions of pages. It seems inconceivable, but when you actually look at a big site and think of how many pages it takes to list thousands of products for sale or present technical support articles or archive news stories, it begins to seem more credible.

The sheer proliferation of information, and the variety of ways in which you can get at it, makes it hard to judge at a glance whether sites are really of any interest to you.[2] Knowing a little more about how potential employers are presenting themselves on the web, for example, can help. So here's a quick guide to some of the different kinds of websites you might come across in your search for a new job. In the next chapter, you'll find other parts of the internet beyond the world wide web.

1 How do the major recruitment sites work? **pages 4–5, Chapter 2 and 3, page 59.**
2 How can I tell which sites are the best to use? **page 24, pages 30–31.**

Brochureware: this is a term often used disparagingly to describe sites which simply present information about a company, i.e. an online 'brochure'. When businesses first began to wake up to the internet as a medium for promotion (which in Britain was not that long ago), this kind of site was all the rage, and there are still a lot of them about. Often this means dry and dull pages of worthy text, but some of it might be useful to you as a jobseeker.

The giants: in the same way that a handful of giant publishing houses have come to dominate the book market, or the computer software world, certain firms have inevitably had the resources to create bigger and better sites than their competitors. Even if you know you don't want to work for the dominators in your particular area of interest, you would probably do well to check out their web presence. Content rules these days, and these are the people who can afford to provide it. Smaller firms often need to justify content by the revenue it might bring them and therefore demand that you pay for a password to access their archives, for example. Many larger sites just put everything out there for the world to see – because they can. Look out for specialist news services, for example.[3]

Portals: the unique thing about the web is that it enables lesser players to strike it rich by offering services that cut out the hassle for users. Searching for information is an art in itself, but what if someone is offering to save you the bother by gathering together information on your behalf? This is what the portals do. Popular sites such as *www.freeserve.net* and *www.yahoo.com* work in this way (as well as offering broader search facilities): go to their homepages, and you will see collections of links to other sites.

These are not just any old sites, though: larger portals sell space to these sites, and there's often a huge commercial deal lurking behind them. If you're a jobhunter and you go to Freeserve, for example, you'll see a link to a Careers 'channel', with links within that to around half a dozen job-related sites. Why those sites? Remember that the portal has decided this on your behalf (and probably to its own advantage) – they might be useful to you, they might not. The problem with portals is that your choices are being narrowed rather than broadened. The idea behind all this of course is that you will go back to the portal for your various needs rather than going directly to the sites themselves, even though, ultimately, all the portal does is take you there anyway. It's often more convenient … and it enables large amounts of advertising to be wafted past your gaze en route.

Web logs: these are related to portals in that they redirect you elsewhere, although they are usually much simpler. A web log is really nothing more than a list of links

---

3 How can I find the news in a particular industry? **pages 20–21, pages 138–140.**

selected by whoever runs it, with the significant additional factor that it is usually updated frequently, even every hour. People across the net use them to let others know what they're up to, which interesting sites they have come across, and so on. Again, you're relying on someone else's choices and judgements, but nevertheless they do offer a useful way of getting round the net quickly and getting to hear about things that you might not otherwise have come across. They are only going to be a tangential way of looking for jobs, however: all you are likely to find is the occasional site with one individual's recommendation. For more information, have a look at *www.weblogs.com*.

Communities: this term can mean a lot of things on the web, and really just signifies any form of site or sites where people with shared needs or interests can gather in some way to exchange ideas and information. A good example of a broad community is a web ring (*see* panel below). More localised communities can be found within sites: Monster, for example, has communities ranging from recent graduates to local government and learning and training, which bring together resources, articles, links and company profiles relevant to the particular theme.[4]

_____ Of rings **and links** _____

The web thrives on communication and sites offering through-routes to other sites. There are two terms you may come across this area:

- ☞ **web rings** are simply groups of separate websites, where the people who run them have agreed to form a loose alliance; from one member site, you can get to any other quickly;

- ☞ a **link exchange** is a site, or a part of a site, which contains a collection of links – often advertised with graphics or banner ads as well as mere lists of text – to a variety of other sites; any one site A links to will also have a link back to that site A, although unlike a web ring, sites B and C might well not have links to each other.

One of the main benefits for the people who run these sites is that links increase traffic and are often used as an index of popularity, therefore leading to better placings in some search engine results. For the user, they offer a quick way to find sites quite closely related to the one you're already looking at.

4 What other kinds of internet community are there? **Chapter 5.**

Jobsites: in this book this term is used to mean any site that maintains a database of jobs which you as a jobhunter can search through. Within this definition, there are various models.

 Sites for **sore eyes**

Jobsites can vary in terms of both the ground they cover and the people who are behind them. In the first case, you can come across:

☞ catch-all sites claiming to cover every type of job imaginable;

☞ all-industry sites targeted at particular levels of experience;

☞ niche sites covering purely a particular industry or field.

Let's look at some examples. In the first case, *www.totaljobs.com* and *www.gisajob.com* would be good examples – the former, for example, covers sectors as diverse as science, secretarial and forestry.

A site which targets a particular kind of worker across a variety of fields is *www.topjobs.co.uk*. In effect, even if they do not state the case as clearly as Topjobs, a lot of the main jobsites that you'll have heard of tend primarily to address the white collar graduate markets as their main focus. A site such as *www.cityjobs.com* combines this white collar target market with a focus on particular sectors, in this case finance, media and IT.

Niche sites will be covered in more detail shortly, but suffice it to say here that using them is a great way to know that you're not going to be inundated with huge numbers of jobs that are definitely of no interest to you.

As for the people behind the sites you see, again there are different players, and here in particular it is often quite difficult to find out who they really are. Some possibilities are:

☞ pure 'dot com' companies with no prior recruitment experience;

☞ recruitment agencies putting some or all of their vacancies on the net;

☞ dot coms with backing from large employers, which may be agencies.

You've got good reason to be interested in this issue. Unfortunately sites that fall into the first category are by far the most common. They're probably the most likely to go under, too. From your point of view, even if you prefer not to go through recruitment agencies, you are at least going to get a better product from sites which do actually know the business. Recruitment agencies are sometimes just go-betweens matching candidates to vacancies with little experience of the job-related issues involved, but as often as not they're trained professionals who really know the business itself as much as how to get you and employers together. If you're reading an online article about how to write a CV, you're far better off knowing that whoever wrote it actually reads CVs for a living. That could mean they're an employer themselves, or a good agency.

Internet recruitment has been a highly controversial area for many agencies, and large numbers of them have resented the intrusion of high-speed start-ups with no relevant experience on their turf. But the tide is already there – people like you are expecting things of the internet, and it's up to them to realise that. The best and most well-known agencies have already done so, and more and more of them are getting their act together on the net. You should expect to be able to go to a recruitment consultant's website and find more than just brochureware these days: what you want is to be able to look through what they've got available.

Some of the biggest jobsites have indeed got professional recruiters behind them, although it's not always immediately obvious. Monster, for example, is part of TMP Worldwide, which is one of the world's largest recruitment agencies, while Totaljobs is part of the Reed group. Yet Reed also has a large, more direct presence on the net at *www.reed.co.uk*. Why would it differentiate like this? Part of the answer is to divide and conquer. A separate, internet-only division allows for marketing to be aimed at people who think first of the internet; the main site, associated with the Reed Worldwide group of recruitment consultancies, then catches people who are more used to going to the agencies. The actual source might be the same (well, broadly: separate brands often have a lot of autonomy), but it's tailored to your particular interests, and that's no bad thing. The penthouse jacuzzi and the school showers probably get their water from the same reservoir … but you know which one you prefer to use when you want a wash.

_____ Who owns **a site?** _____

Sometimes you may feel you want to know just a little bit more about a site than is immediately obvious. There are two useful methods:

☞ look for an 'About us' section on the site, where you may find details of parent companies, affiliates, or even company reports and trading information;

☞ go to *www.register.com* and type in the site address. It will say it is taken, of course, and you can then follow the link to see who owns it. Not every company reveals full details, however.

_____ Niche to **see you** _____

There are hundreds of recruitment firms in this country, and hundreds of recruitment websites. Not all of them are in the catch-all game: many make a healthy living from specialising. But it can be a problem tracking them down. If you don't know of any useful starting points, it's a good idea to ask around (and you can read all about doing that on the internet in the next chapter) plus you can approach it from two angles.

The first is to flex your internet search muscles and try to narrow down the flood of information you get on the search engines, then take a look at the panel overleaf for some specific tips.[5]

5 How do I narrow down search results? **pages 22–23.**

_____ Find **your niche** _____

Here are some good ways to track down niche recruitment sites:

☞ use the search engines effectively – think of more than one aspect of your quarry, then insist that any results must contain both: **healthcare AND managerial**, say;

☞ try *www.agencycentral.co.uk* – this has helpful lists of recruitment agencies and their websites by sector;

☞ do a search at *www.onrec.com* – it's a specialist magazine all about online recruitment, and often has news about specific sites;

☞ try a big directory such as Yahoo! – look from both ends, i.e. the *sector*, where jobs may be a subcategory, and *jobs/careers*, where the sector may be a subcategory.

The second is to find out who the bricks-and-mortar agencies are and then see if they have websites. Once you've got a name it's usually not that hard to find a site on the net. And finding a name? Here it gets more difficult. On the internet it's easy to find lists of general recruitment sites, but there is inevitably less demand for lists of specialists given that you're probably only going to use them once. However free services on the internet look, the sad and cynical truth is that a lot of them only offer a service through which they can sell advertising. And how many advertisers are going to be keen on sites that only get one visit?

So remember the old ways again: pick up the *Yellow Pages* (although you can also search it at *www.yell.com*), go to the local library careers centre, or to a specialist careers library. Where can you find those? Take a look at *www.prospects.csu.ac.uk/student/cidd/carserv/index.htm* for a start.

Businesses of all kinds are realising that they can offer powerful and useful services with fairly minimal costs on the internet, so you'll find that the specialists are definitely out there. Another good place to try is publishing firms.

'Old media' publishers of all shapes and sizes have been dealt a few body blows by the internet, but they've also been quick to jump on the bandwagon. If you're a graduate, you'll probably have been to *www.jobsunlimited.com*, the *Guardian*'s jobsite. In one of the first moments in *The Rebel*, the film mentioned in Chapter 2, the camera lingers on a plat-form poster reading 'Better jobs in the *Evening Standard*'. Now you can find the same paper's vacancies at *www.BigBlueDog.com*. The big papers have even got together in sur-prising partnerships: *www.fish4jobs.com*, for example, is the brainchild of unlikely bedfel-lows such as Trinity Mirror (publishers of the *Daily Mirror*) and Northcliffe (*Daily Mail*), as well as various regional newspaper groups.

The same principle applies to the more specialist press. If you know there's a maga-zine or newspaper in your field, look it up on the web, and you might find not only that they've got a useful and informative site but that they've also realised that recruitment is where it's at. Let's take an example.

If you're looking for work as the manager of a care home, there are only a couple of magazines that you might read. Pick up your copy of the *Caring Times* (we're not making this up) and you'll find a website from the same company is advertised: *www.careinfo.org*. This site has been set up to provide a one-stop resource for anyone working in the long-term care sector. As well as providing an archive of relevant news stories, which you might find useful to help you learn more about big companies operating in the field plus any political issues you need to know about, there's a recruitment section. This follows a familiar model: you can search for jobs by category and location, and you can also follow links to read company profiles about particular employers.[6]

Supposing this is a move in a different direction for you and you don't yet know about the *Caring Times*. How would you find this site? Well, one obvious answer is to ask around – get in touch with people doing the job, and find out what they read. But unless you've got contacts, that kind of cold calling often isn't easy, or indeed welcome. If you can find the names of companies, you could probably e-mail them: that's a much easier way of getting in touch on spec, as people have the option of ignoring it without being rude if they really don't want to know. A speculative e-mail to *info@bigcorp.com* might go astray – but you'll soon be told if it has (it will 'bounce back' to your inbox, with a technical message which might explain why).[7]

If this proves a problem, then once again you need to tackle the search engines. There are niche sites for all kinds of sectors (IT? Try *www.techcareers.com*. Catering? How about *www.foodjobs.co.uk*. Want some part-time work while you search for your dream job? Drink in *www.barzone.co.uk*.) – you just need to learn to find them.

---

6 What are company profiles? **page 24.**
7 How do I find someone's e-mail address? **page 27.**

The Monster guide
to finding a job abroad

Ben Giddings of Monster.co.uk writes:

☞ Start with a jobsite that you trust in your own country and see if it has an international network. Monster has sites throughout Europe, North America and the Pacific Rim for example. If not, try going via specialist industry sector sites. If a field is quite specialised, they often give details of working further afield simply because a specialised industry sector needs to be more flexible towards international movement in order to meet recruitment demands.

☞ Just as important as finding the vacancy though is getting background information on the country – culture, laws, healthcare system, welfare, etc. Often, people who are looking to work abroad know quite a bit about their industry sector, but very little about the countries they are considering a move to. Have a look at *www.expatnetwork.co.uk*, which offers good basic background info on countries for prospective employees and is a good starting point for finding out if you actually want to work in the country. Other sites to investigate are *www.globalnetwork.co.uk* and *www.escapeartist.com*. And if you want to travel as you work, check out the resources at *www.transabroad.com*.

☞ One thing to be aware of, however, is applying for jobs with employers who don't want overseas candidates. Discriminatory or not, some employers just aren't interested in overseas candidates, having not yet cast their nets in international waters, and will blatantly say so on their advertisements. But that doesn't stop people applying, which just annoys them. There's no telling some people!

Using an overseas jobsite is dead easy. Web professional Paul Notley, for example, moved from working in a UK call centre to a life of sun and surf in California: 'I found a position at *www.dice.com* and followed the link to the company's website, where I got the contact information and applied by e-mailing my resume and a covering letter – I was then interviewed by phone.'[8]

---

8 Any advice on telephone interviews? **pages 127–128.**

_____ Remote **possibilities** _____

Delving further into the realm of niche sites, we can now consider specialist ways of working as well as specialist fields. Many kinds of work have opened up to allow workers much more flexible lifestyles, particularly in the media and the internet.

If you're considering a freelance career, for example, it's easy to feel a little isolated once you've shrugged off the warm embrace of full-time employment. Where can you turn? Again, there are various paths you can follow:

- searching through catch-all jobsites;
- websites associated with relevant magazines;
- dedicated sites for freelancers.

The first route is unlikely to come up with much: freelance work by its very nature is quite difficult to pin down, and it's often not worth the bother for broad websites and agencies to deal with it. You can try using the major jobsites, but the truth is that unless they are advertising this kind of work in their databases, it's unlikely you'll come up with much. But why not set up a couple of spare search agents just in case?

> **❝'Telework' as we traditionally think of it is morphing into a broader form of remote access or mobile work. What the internet has done has been to provide a common information access point for mobile workers so they can do a great deal of their 'office work' away from the office.❞**
>
> Gil Gordon, global telecommuting expert, Gil Gordon Associates

Again, turning to the existing press is a good start, not only to learn about the joys and pitfalls of a more independent career but also to find useful online arenas. Magazines such as _Working From Home_ (_www.home-workers.com_) offer a selection of articles, plus discussion areas for the exchange of ideas and information.

And there are a number of specialist sites. If you're looking for freelance design, writing or web work, for example, check out _www.freelancers.net_. This site gives you your own 'homepage' under its umbrella, where you can display career history details, a portfolio perhaps, and what you're looking for. If you'd rather not be shepherded into using a restricted format, there's the option to use yourname.freelancers.net to take viewers directly to a page you've designed for yourself elsewhere – and they don't even need to see the 'real' address (this is useful if you're using a free web space service, for example, where the URL might be long and unmemorable).[9]

The more you get your name in circulation in ways like this, the more you'll find unexpected nuggets of opportunity landing unsolicited in your e-mail inbox.[10]

_____ Go to work **on the web** _____

According to the Office of National Statistics, around a quarter of a million people became teleworkers between spring 1999 and spring 2000, by which time 5.5 per cent of the UK workforce was working from home at least one day a week. This is just the people using PCs and telecoms. Of these, 27 per cent are in business or financial services, and most are managers or professionals of some kind. Check out these links for more about the teleworking revolution:

- ☞ *www.wfh.co.uk* – British Telecom's dedicated teleworking site (guess who stands to gain from lots of people using the phone and the internet);
- ☞ *www.emergence.nu* – all about changes in global working practices;
- ☞ *www.telework2000.com* – a conference held last year and endorsed by the Prime Minister on the homepage;
- ☞ *www.tca.org.uk* – the Telework Association;
- ☞ *www.eto.org.uk* – European Telework Online's site includes a useful list of teleworkers' jobsites, with comments on their usefulness.

_____ Thumbing **the directories** _____

Another area of the internet we have only touched on so far is information resources, i.e. sites that might not have any direct involvement with recruitment but provide general services that you might find useful. These might not directly get you a job, but they can certainly help you stay informed, and will often link to other sites that you can bookmark.

9 How do I create a homepage? **pages 51–53.**
10 How do I filter my e-mail? **page 142.**

Some of these are effectively portals by another name.[11] Check out *www.thebiz.com*, for example, which brings together links to a wide variety of business-to-business services, including recruiters. You'll also find links to online training resources here.[12]

_____ Sic but **true** _____

You'd be surprised by how mistyping names into your browser can take you far away from where you want to go. Typing *www.the-biz.com* (with hyphen) instead of *www.thebiz.com* (without), for example, takes you to a communications group in the States. Now and again there's even a faint chance that serendipity could take you somewhere really useful, but it's unlikely. The most common reality is that unless firms have had the sense to buy up domain names similar to their main one, rivals or other malefactors are likely to have got there.

The directory-based search engines such as Yahoo! and Excite can help in this respect: travel down through the 'Business' or 'Jobs' branches and you can find categorised lists of sites with a brief one-line description for each. Remember, these sites often have a UK version (e.g. *http://uk.yahoo.com*) which you can usually find or be redirected to by typing .co.uk at the end instead of .com.

_____ Life not as **we know it** _____

The internet as we use it at the moment is already being challenged by other forms of presentation, so it's worth staying up with the technology. Any medium that proves a success is bound to attract the interest of recruiters, and that means it could be of use to you.

Mobile phones, for example, have become a major focus for internet content through the WAP system. WAP is effectively a set of codes (otherwise known as a 'protocol', which is what the 'p' stands for, the rest of it being 'wireless application') which enable simplified web pages to be displayed on the much smaller screen of a mobile phone.

11 What are portals? **page 57.**
12 What online training resources are there? **pages 147–150.**

For content providers, the challenge is to find ways of presenting the information and services they supply to match the medium. For you, it means you've got another way of occupying yourself on long train journeys (tunnels permitting).

Why bother? The answer to this depends on how many providers adopt this medium, of course, and in the case of WAP almost the moment it arrived in the high street the 'third generation' of similar technology was announced. You can keep up with the news at *www.wap-mag.co.uk*. But it already offers a lot of potential, particularly when related to our good old friends the search agents. If you're in a competitive industry, what better way to give you an edge than instant access to vacancies as they come up – your search agent can send a text message directly to your mobile, for instance.

A number of recruiters are offering WAP jobsearch facilities. David Brown of *www.gisajob.com*, which was the first jobsite in the UK to offer this service, enthuses: 'Since signing up with BT Cellnet to provide job content for their WAP portal, we've had an ever-increasing amount of traffic to the site. We're now moving into phase two of their rollout of WAP technology.' Recruitment firm Antal International was also quick to get involved, signing an agreement with mobile phone provider Nokia – *see www.antal.com/wap* for details. Stepstone offers both search agents and job category searches by WAP, which will send employer contact details direct to your phone; Topjobs and Monster meanwhile have forged an alliance with *www.yac.com* so that travelling job-hunters can receive voice messages by e-mail. It's hard to keep up with the pace of change.

If you're looking for sites of all kinds to play with on your WAP-enabled handset, the definitive site to go to is *www.wap.com*, which includes a wide variety of background information, plus a comprehensive directory of WAP websites.

> **❝The internet is extending beyond computers into other platforms, and the most interesting of these so far are the mobile ones. I can see its value if you need information urgently, wherever you may be. For the foreseeable future, however, I still think the computer platform is the easiest for undertaking in-depth research.❞**
>
> Tom Campbell, futurologist, New Media Knowledge

The popularity of the internet has soared in the course of only a few years, but it still remains limited by the primary means by which we access it, namely the desktop computer. The truth is that however PC literate we are as a nation, and particularly in the workplace, the number of people who own a PC (let alone WAP phones) is still in a minority, albeit a large and growing one. The mighty corporations wishing to reach us through the net as well as all their other tentacles are keen to improve upon this, and thus they are turning to the one medium to which almost everyone still succumbs to some extent – television. Digital TV is now with us, and according to Forrester Research, interactive digital TV (iDTV) will be in 50 per cent of European households by 2005 and is likely to become 'the major point of online access', with 200 000 new users already signing up every month (*source:* Jobchannel.tv).

For anyone who's an enthusiast about the internet, in some senses this spells bad news: TV, however 'interactive' it becomes, is a 'push' medium, i.e. one that feeds you, the drooling viewer, with material. The PC-based internet is generally more 'pull'-orientated: you have to solicit things by going out there and looking for them. This might mean a little more effort, but it also means more choice than the 'walled garden' approach of the digital networks, which are likely to be dominated by a handful of players.

That caveat aside, TV is an obvious choice for recruiters, and you should keep an eye on your options there as much as anywhere else.[13] There is already a dedicated digital TV channel exclusively for jobhunters – Jobchannel.tv. It seems unlikely that the big web recruitment players will let themselves be left behind – they are all now conspicuously vying for attention in ad breaks on terrestrial TV as it is.

The race to take charge of the digital TV market has already begun, in fact. Multi-media TV has launched the Job Channel on the Open network, and there's another recruitment channel on the Sky Digital network, which includes trade news from different sectors as well as job opportunities. The top websites are joining in: customers of the NTL cable network can access jobs from Stepstone, for example. There are other solutions around, too, which aim to bring the simplicity of TV to the diversity of the web: have a look at *www.myturninc.com*.

The good thing about the computer-based internet is that in the bizarrely ephemeral terms of our times it is long-lived, and people have devoted huge amounts of time and resources to make it work. If you can think of it, it's there somewhere. So what you need to do now is go out and meet some kindred spirits …

---

13 What else does the future hold? **Chapter 10.**

———— Time to **try it out** ————

Use the panel on finding niche sites in this chapter to do just that: what field do you work in at the moment? Do you know any sites? See if you can find any others: these might come in useful in your job right now.

————————————————————————

CHAPTER FIVE

Meet the people

How to communicate **on the net**

The whole internet is buzzing with conversation. Some of it may well be about *Star Trek*, but a lot of it's also about people learning from each other

Although all you need to get a new job might well be setting up carefully tailored search agents[1] and an online CV,[2] together with mastering the dark art of search engines[3] so you can always get hold of the information you need whenever you need it, you're still going to be in the running alongside a lot of other people. Jobhunting is inevitably a competitive business, and anything that can help you stay ahead of the pack has got to be good. It's time to think laterally.

This chapter will offer some alternative routes to take in the pursuit of your twin quarries of gathering information and finding a job. You may not need them, and if so all well and good, but if your agents and your enquiries are still not bearing fruit, then you might need to be more adventurous.

One of the noticeable characteristics of jobhunting on the net is that it offers a lot of comfort and very little challenge. It can be quite fun surfing away hiding in the wings,

1 How *do* I carefully tailor my search agents? **pages 36–37.**
2 What's the best way to approach an online CV? **page 40, page 103.**
3 What are the necessary incantations? **pages 22–23.**

safe in front of your terminal. But if you really want a new job, at some point you're going to have to talk to people:

☞ prospective employers

☞ recruitment consultants

☞ people working in your chosen field

☞ people who might know any of the above.

The internet is about communication as much as information.

_____ Looking **for guidance** _____

When, at the age of 35, Dante set out through the woods and entered on his life-transforming voyage through hell and beyond, he didn't go it alone: Virgil was there to guide him.

The search for a new job is a time when the spotlight is thrown on your abilities, and however confident you may be, it can be very valuable to get in touch with people who know what they're talking about, especially if you're planning a change of direction.[4] This is something that the better jobsites have already been addressing, although at the moment it's only commercially viable for them to go so far. For you as a career seeker, your ideal would be to have one-to-one, expert advice on the internet whenever you need it, for free. But careers advisers, like you, have to earn a living.

Nevertheless, there really are people out there who, when it's convenient at least, will listen to your questions and do their best to answer them. At *www.monster.co.uk*, for example, you will find a dedicated Career Centre. You may have already paid a few brief visits to it in the course of researching companies and employment markets, but there's also an 'Ask an expert' section. At the time of writing, experts are available in more than a dozen categories, some of them for general issues such as writing your CV and interview techniques,[5] plus wider concerns such as employment for disabled people, equal opportunities[6] and so on, and others who focus on particular industries such as technology or the automotive sector. Two of the most popular areas are equal opportunities and career change.

4 How do I assess my abilities? **page 115.**
5 How should I prepare for interviews? **pages 122–125.**
6 Where do I find out about general employment issues? **page 152.**

But what does 'available' actually mean? In Monster's model, they are accessible via 'message boards'. These consist of forms on the website (rather than, say, e-mail) whereby you can type in a query, which will then be posted up on their particular page. This means that whatever you're discussing is inherently public: you can see what others have been asking, and they can see your questions, too.

While this means that there are certain more specific issues that you might not want to discuss, especially if you're accessing the web from work,[7] it does have the advantage that you can learn from other people's questions, which might be things that it hadn't occurred to you to ask.

The experts themselves, who are indeed experts, in Monster's case either running their own companies or working for the recruitment giant TMP Worldwide, undertake to read the messages at least twice a week and, where possible, offer a helpful reply. A biography of each expert is provided so you know just how qualified they really are.[8]

> **"We like questions which allow us to give impartial advice, using our specialist knowledge. Best ones are those which we can reply to succinctly without having to resort to *War and Peace*, where we can refer jobhunters to the best place to find information they are seeking. It's also good to receive questions which challenge and make us think, and those which open up a debate."**
>
> Beth Cauldwell, Monster.co.uk expert from TMP Worldwide

At the moment, those sites which offer this kind of dedicated service are very much in the minority, and one reason must surely be that so many sites are set up by internet experts rather than professional recruiters. A refreshing change from that, however, is *www.gradunet.co.uk*, which has a 'virtual career office' – in other words, a web forum.[9] Those who don't like washing their dirty laundry in public, however, will be reassured by the words of Beth Cauldwell of TMP Worldwide, who is one of the experts at Monster.co.uk: 'Message boards are great as a forum, but for anyone who is actively looking for a career move it is always useful to e-mail or call the recruiter for a private consultation.'

7 Can I get in trouble for doing this? **pages 140–141.**
8 Who writes the articles that appear on jobsites? **pages 19–20 and 24.**
9 Where can I find real careers offices? **page 62.**

_____ Forum or **against 'em** _____

These communities of experts form a good example of how some of the one-stop jobsites really are worth going back to over and over again. But you don't have to stop there alone. The whole internet is buzzing with conversation. Some of it may well be about *Star Trek*, but a lot of it's also about people learning from each other: sharing experiences, developing skills, keeping up with their field.

If you've been using search engines in depth, you may have noticed that sometimes when you search for something quite specific, what comes up is not a website as such but rather a 'thread' in a message board discussion. What's a thread? You can see them in those Monster expert message boards: if the expert responds to your question, then someone else asks another question partly in response to that, i.e. under the same subject heading, you've got yourself a thread. On some sites you can 'subscribe' to these threads so that you can read the latest on a specific debate whenever someone posts a new message.

If you hit upon a thread in your search results, it's worth going both down the tree to see if anything else of interest has been said on whatever theme it's about, and up the tree to the 'parent' discussion. You might well have found a specialist discussion board that you might not have come across otherwise.

That's all very well, of course, but happening upon things at random is not really the kind of advice you were probably looking for. So where do you go to find specific discussion groups? The answer is:

☞ everywhere you've looked already;

☞ specialist search engines.

The first point might seem a bit glib, but the chances are that if you've been researching things in the way this book has been encouraging you to, you'll almost certainly have come across discussion groups of relevance to you already, not just on the large jobsites but also in niche areas, resource centres, everywhere. If you see any of these terms:

☞ forum

☞ message board

☞ bulletin board

☞ discussion group

you'll have found the same sort of animal. Take a look, ask questions, get involved.

_____ Everybody's **talking** _____

And now for specialist search engines. Point your browser to *www.forumone.com*, for example, and you'll find a site dedicated purely to helping you track down web forums on anything and everything. Search for 'jobs' and you'll get a list of more than 500!

Naturally, 500 is probably more than 490 too many as far as you're concerned, and a subject such as 'jobs' is almost certainly too general. This is one instance when narrowing your search is what's called for. Let's go back to the good old example of marine biology: if you just type in 'marine biology', you'll still get literally hundreds of responses, as the results throw up anything with 'marine' OR 'biology' in their subject descriptions. So you need an 'advanced search', which should have its own link.[10] Now you can type 'marine AND biology', and this time you'll probably get around 20 hits. That's much more manageable.

Many of the larger and most popular portals host their own discussion groups, too. Check out *www.clubs.yahoo.com*, for example – filling in a quick registration form will give you access to hundreds of discussion areas, including marine biology.

_____ Register **this** _____

You may be wondering with some jobsites and other services on the web whether you should bother to register your details. For one thing, there are security issues.[11] If you have found a jobsite that seems to offer what you want, then yes, you will probably benefit from registering, as that will mean you can set up complex search agents and use facilities which will clearly benefit you.

If you can try things out online first, then all well and good; if not, consider why they're so keen to get your personal details. Some sites give you the option of how much information you want to disclose. For example, Monster.co.uk allows you to save an inactive CV which you can use to apply for jobs but recruiters cannot access; save a CV as confidential and apply for jobs without disclosing your personal details; or have your entire CV open to anyone. Always read the small print to be on the safe side. Many sites of all kinds can lead to you being bombarded with unwanted e-mails if you're not careful[12] – look for checkboxes which give you

---

10 What about advanced techniques with general search engines? **pages 22–23.**
11 Can anyone access my personal details? **this page and page 86.**
12 How do I cut down the junk mail? **page 144.**

> the chance to decline receiving further messages.[13] In Britain, sites are obliged to give you this option under the data protection laws.
>
> Independent careers consultant Sue Hodgson says: 'Avoid *any* site which tries to extract a registration fee from you.'

Having looked at a few of these discussion sites, you may be thinking to yourself that they are all very well, but most of them are in America, say, or full of people discussing how to tell one type of coral from another rather than how to get a job as a marine biologist. Both of these objections may be true, but they are easily answered. These discussion forums are really worldwide, however US-based they might appear to be. People in other countries are probably asking the same questions as you, and the answers will probably still be very pertinent.

It's also pretty easy to make sure that you're only looking at UK-based sites if that really is an issue for you. In the case of Yahoo!, you can even go to *http://uk.clubs.yahoo.com*. As for the subject matters under discussion, it's up to you to steer things round. Posting a new question doesn't mean it has to fit in with what's already there: if you've got something to ask, then go ahead and ask it. It's unlikely that people will mind.

❝Be careful with user names. It's all very funny calling yourself 'Ladykiller', but you wouldn't introduce yourself at an interview like that, so don't do it online where thousands of employers can see you.❞

Ben Giddings, content manager, Monster.co.uk

This point can be enlarged, of course: if no one out there really seems to be discussing your area of interest (although that seems unlikely), you can simply start your own forum. If you think that sounds like a lot of effort, it isn't. The advantage of sites such as Yahoo! Clubs (check out *www.egroups.com*, too) is that they do the actual hosting. They'll moderate for abusive language, and all you have to do is start the ball rolling. If you want

13 Tell me more about filling in online forms, **page 39.**

to stay more involved, you can. All the technology is so automated that it really is just a question of posting messages when you feel like it, which could be only once or numerous times.

_____ Become **a groupie** _____

The forums discussed above are web-based – if you are surfing from home, you might be put off therefore by the online time taken to compose your messages. It is often possible to save your phone bills by surfing off-line to some extent (see panel below), but you still need to be online to send your message and read whatever other people have posted in response. So is there anything that isn't web-based?

_____ Off-line **browsing** _____

Although in theory the internet offers quick access to information, you can still amass a huge phone bill when all the hours add up. There are two ways in which you can improve this situation:

☞ *Use the 'browse off-line' option in your browser*
Access the pages you want to see as normal, but don't sit there and read them while you're on the phone. Go through the pages you want to read quickly, then disconnect from the phone and select off-line browsing, usually found under the File menu. You can now surf through those pages at your leisure and without being on the phone. If you find only some of them have been saved before the browser asks you to connect to the net again, go to the options or preferences menu and make your 'cache' bigger – this is the part of your PC's memory where those web pages are stored. One note, though: making it too big will slow down the overall performance of your browser.

☞ *Use a dedicated off-line browser program*
There are various programs available, such as Web Buddy and Pagesucker, which allow you to name a site and how many levels of pages you want to

grab. The program then goes online, saves all that information as quickly as possible and disconnects so that you can have an entire site stored on your hard drive, although you're better off not going through too many levels, or it will still take ages. Think of how big most sites are when you take into account how many other pages each page can link to.[14] In Internet Explorer, you can add a page to your Favourites list, then choose 'Make available off-line' to achieve the same effect.

The format adopted by the web-based message boards is modelled very closely on an older part of the internet (in the true sense of the word rather than its common conflation with just the web), namely newsgroups. Also known as Usenet, these too are discussion groups, conducted with little concern for geography and bringing together people with all manner of interests, but you don't need to be surfing the world wide web to use them.

Newsgroups offer the same diversity as web-based forums – there are well over 60 000 newsgroups to date – and when you set up your PC appropriately, they can be much quicker. There are reasons why the web is taking over this kind of communication, however: to take advantage of that extra speed and convenience, a certain amount of setting up is required. The good news is that it's no harder than getting your e-mail software to work.

The most widely used web browsers will allow you to access newsgroups through them anyway – all you need are the details from your ISP of something called your 'news server', analogous to the 'mail server' which you'll have used to set up your e-mail account, unless, that is, you're using a web-based e-mail account such as Hotmail (*see* panel opposite). You can set all this up through the News link in the Preferences menu of your browser.

Another issue is the atmosphere of the community: newsgroups tend to attract slightly more hardcore enthusiasts. This means that if you find a group in your sought-after subject area, you're likely to find some real experts, but they can sometimes be a little unforgiving. There are important security issues, too, which we'll come to.[15]

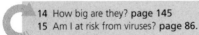

14 How big are they? **page 145**
15 Am I at risk from viruses? **page 86.**

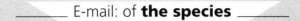

_____ E-mail: of **the species** _____

People often don't realise that there are two main types of e-mail. The first, **POP3** (SMTP effectively works in a similar way, if you hear that mentioned), is the kind you check with a special program, such as Eudora, Pegasus or Outlook Express, although in the case of the latter it's most often used as part of a package with Internet Explorer; Netscape Communicator also allows you to send and receive this kind of e-mail.

To use 'real e-mail', you need to set up that program with various bits of information, primarily the name/s of your incoming and outgoing mail servers – all this is information which your ISP will supply. The advantage of this kind of mail is that it's quick, and you can read and write as many messages as you want off-line, as well as filter them and all sorts.[16] The disadvantage is that the PC you're using needs to be configured with all this information, which usually isn't practical at work, for example.[17]

Webmail has been immortalised by Hotmail, which used to be an independent company but was bought out by Microsoft. Webmail enables you to send and receive messages through a website, which of course you can access from anywhere in the whole wide world that has web access. It's a good idea to set up a spare account like this – generally, you only have to use it once every three months to keep the account active anyway. What will keep it active for you, however, is most likely all the junk mail you'll get.[18]

In these days of New Labour, there is in fact now a 'third way' of sorts: some webmail accounts (Hotmail included) actually allow you to check a POP mail account through the site. Just follow the 'Get POP' link in the case of Hotmail, and you can type in your mail server information (for several accounts, in fact) to check your mail, which will remain on the mail server for you to download it at home, too. A word of warning, though: do you really want to type your private user name and password into a website, however secure it is?

16 How can I organise my e-mails better? **page 142.**
17 What other issues are there re surfing at work? **pages 140–141.**
18 What is spam and how do I stop it? **page 88, page 144.**

If all this is sounding rather scary, you can either phone your internet service provider's helpline and they should be able to provide a fairly painless way of setting all this up, or you can stick to the web. If you look at *www.deja.com/usenet*, you can not only search for newsgroups of interest but also view their content through the web. It's slower than direct access, but at least it's no different from normal surfing. Note that the Deja search engine will actually search individual postings for your query: if you just type in 'jobs', this time you can expect around 50 000 hits!

If your curiosity has been piqued, however, by far the best thing to do is use a dedicated newsreader program – there are plenty of them available for free for all platforms, and you'll usually find some on the cover disks of the popular internet magazines. A newsreader works in a similar way to e-mail programs such as Outlook Express or Eudora: you can access the groups, read messages off-line having downloaded them to your computer, and post messages back whenever you feel like it, all the while minimising your time on the telephone.

If you've decided to give newsgroups a try, and you're not going via the web-only route, you need to begin by downloading a list of groups. Given the number out there, this can take at least 15 minutes, although it depends on the news server you're using, as different ISPs permit you to access different groups. It's unlikely that you'll be able to get at all of them, and there's a good reason for this: an unfortunately high percentage of 'Usenet space' is devoted to pornography. If there happens to be a perfectly respectable group that you can't get through your ISP, you can usually request that they enable you to access it.

_____ Groups **of groups** _____

Newsgroups are very much known by their names. Here are some of the prefixes that might be of most use to you, the jobseeker:

- ☞ **alt.** – covers all manner of areas, including many free discussions;
- ☞ **biz.** – postings related to the world of commerce;
- ☞ **soc.** – social and cultural discussions;
- ☞ **sci.** – science (see also **bionet**);
- ☞ **uk.** – stay within this green and pleasant land.

There are many newsgroups which might be of interest to you. Some of the more well-known ones in the jobs arena (though be warned, the more general a site, the bigger it is, which means it can take ages to download even just the headers of all the messages) are:

- biz.jobs.offered
- misc.jobs.offered
- uk.jobs.offered
- uk.jobs.wanted.

In general, your best bet is to download the list of newsgroups available to you and then search for the word 'jobs', for example. That should bring up a range of more specific sites, too.

The groups themselves are categorised within their names: each has a prefix which at least gives some indication of where they are based or what sort of subject areas they cover. Check out the panel for a list of the prefixes that are most likely to be of interest to you, the jobseeker. Your newsreader program, by the way, will allow you to search the whole list of available groups for a particular word, which helps track down interesting groups.

_____ The golden rules **of newsgroups** _____

There are two very important things to remember when using newsgroups:

- never download attachments (also called binaries);
- always respect other users.

Newsgroups are in effect a very specific manifestation of e-mail, and when you post a message, your e-mail address will appear next to it (unless you disguise it). This means that you can also send and receive attached files. Don't, don't, don't! Newsgroups are, alas, a very common way for viruses to be transmitted.[19]

19 Tell me more about viruses, **page 86.**

As for respecting other users, that probably seems self-evident to you. But Usenet has a very particular code of conduct. The key points are shown in the guide to 'netiquette' below. If you upset someone unreasonably, you can expect to be 'flamed' with 'spam' (i.e. inundated with huge numbers of junk or abusive e-mails). If that sounds like an unfortunate accident in a meat-processing factory, it's probably not much better. Usenet devotees can be very touchy, and if you offend them they'll offend right back.

There's really no need to be intimidated, though: spam is usually reserved for people who try to post unwanted advertisements in the group, usually of the 'Hey, friend, have you always wanted to earn $10 000 a week?' variety which you're probably familiar with already.

This in itself points to a further warning about Usenet: be careful who you give your e-mail address to. Unscrupulous spammers are always out there 'lurking', compiling huge databases of real people's e-mail addresses so that they can then bombard them with tedious get-rich-quick offers.[20] If you're in any doubt, set up a spare e-mail account purely for Usenet-related use, or lie if you must, like the spammers do themselves. When you set up your newsreader, there's no way anyone can check whether *droopydrawers@sillymail.com* is your real address.

Newsgroup netiquette

- Read the FAQ (frequently asked questions), which is generally posted to the site on a regular basis.

- NEVER USE CAPITAL LETTERS – it's the net equivalent of shouting your head off.

- Don't get involved in arguments.

- Read the other messages first, to make sure your query hasn't already been covered – and make sure the group really is relevant.

20 I'm being bombarded by spam – what can I do? **page 144.**

☞ Keep your messages succinct, and avoid using a long signature (a phrase or set of sentences which you can set up in your e-mail program to be tacked on to the end of every message you send).

☞ Don't repeat too much of the message you're replying to, either: keep it short.

☞ Send replies to the newsgroup address, not to the e-mail address of another message poster (unless you specifically want a private chat).

This section may have seemed quite alarmist, and if you really don't like the sound of Usenet, you're probably better off sticking to the web. But if you're more adventurous, it offers a lot of lateral possibilities: you can really meet some interesting and helpful people out there.

_____ Mail **models** _____

Usenet is not only the alternative manifestation of e-mail: another, extremely useful way of employing it is for mailing lists. These are, as the name suggests, circulars on particular themes that you can choose to subscribe to. There are two main kinds, open and closed. An open list is another form of discussion forum, whereby you can post a message to a dedicated e-mail address (using your normal e-mail program). Your message will then be appended to the list itself, which you and all other subscribers receive by e-mail.

How often you receive messages varies greatly: it might be a daily, weekly or monthly list; you might receive mail every time a new mail has been posted, or maybe once every blue moon. It might well be important to you to find this out: if you sign up gleefully to half a dozen lists, your friends may soon be digging you out of a pile of thousands of largely unwanted e-mails.[21] Don't say you weren't warned!

Closed lists, which can also appear at all manner of time intervals, are simply news services, round-ups of information or whatever that get sent out by whoever runs them. The Monster newsletter is a simple example: once a week you get an e-mail listing any

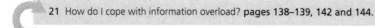

21 How do I cope with information overload? **pages 138–139, 142 and 144.**

new services on the site. Other closed lists do everything from tell you a joke every morning to providing detailed news for a particular industry. There are also a lot of more subversive lists which aim to reveal the underbelly of such worlds. If you want to work in new media or technology, for example, you ought to know about Need to Know: *www.ntk.net*.

How do you find mailing lists? Again, you may well come across them in the course of your cybertravels, but there are also dedicated search engines. The most well known is at *www.liszt.com*, which details nearly 100 000 of them. That sounds a lot, although you'll generally find that mailing lists are much more specific than the other media we've been looking at in this chapter. Your questions and discussions will need to be relevant to the subject or they probably won't get posted.

Most lists are 'moderated', which means there's a human out there somewhere who makes sure that abusive or irrelevant messages don't get on to the list, and who has the right to bring a discussion to a close. The system works, and moderation is best in all things, right?

_____ Mastering the **mailing list** _____

There is one rule above all others that you need to master when using mailing lists, namely the distinction between:

☞ the list's receiving address ('mailing address');

☞ the address associated with the list's actual name (used for admin).

If you want to send a message for public consumption, you must always, repeat always, send it to the former; the latter is the address from which messages are sent. If you want to alter details of your subscription, leave the list or whatever, NEVER send your request to the first address.

In summary: if you want to reply to the list, DON'T just hit reply in your e-mail program. If you want to sort out some admin, DON'T send it to everyone else on the list by mistake!

All mailing lists work in this way, and it's dead easy to follow. If you're in any doubt, almost every mailing list has an associated FAQ message it will send out on request, if it hasn't already done so when you subscribe. FAQ means 'frequently asked questions': the mailing list world is generally a very friendly one, and people have taken the trouble to compile a list of instructions for the novice in this form – all you owe them back is the respect of actually reading it. *www.liszt.com*, the search site for mailing lists, will tell you exactly how to receive the FAQ of a list before you consider subscribing to it.

Some mailing lists even keep **archives** of all messages ever posted to the list, accessible through the list's admin address or an associated website, or both. Read the FAQ or mail the administrator to find out how to access them.

Sometimes there's a **digest** option. This will lump together all the messages from one day, say, or from a week, or whatever is appropriate; like a closed list, it will probably summarise the topics at the beginning, enabling you to save time and read only what interests you. Again, arranging for the digest to be sent instead of each posting one by one is done through the admin address – check the FAQ.

There is one other important sense in which lists can be 'closed', however: not all of them are open to all and sundry who wander by. Liszt, for example, will tell you whether the list is open to public access or not. This isn't as snooty as it sounds: many lists really are set up by private groups for their own discussions, bringing together friends and colleagues across the world in a convenient way, while others might contain confidential discussions that you might have to justify seeing. In general, if you have a legitimate reason to be a subscriber, there shouldn't be a problem, and there'll almost always be a moderator whose e-mail address you can find, to whom you can then appeal.[22]

As with web discussion forums (and newsgroups for that matter, although in this case it's much more complicated), you can set up your own mailing list. It's not quite as simple as creating a web forum, but there are free services, such as *www.listbot.com*, which give you the technology without you having to set up your computer as a permanently online server. The catch is that the free services will almost certainly insist on tacking advertisements on to the end of messages that appear in the list, which might detract from its appeal.

22 How can I find people's e-mail addresses in general? **page 27.**

_____ Internet security – **the issues** _____

Credit card numbers stolen en masse, viruses which destroy your entire hard drive … The tales of data piracy, kidnap and surveillance on the internet would sound at home in the taverns of our seafaring past – and many of them are told to scare rather than to promote the truth. Nevertheless, there are dangers on the net, and according to a survey of internet jobhunters by *www.workthing.com* in spring 2000, only one in eight was going as far as uploading their CV, largely because of worries about confidentiality. So what's the truth, and what can you do?

☞ *Am I at risk from viruses?*

From the world wide web, almost certainly not, even if you're downloading software (though you should always check with antivirus software). From e-mail, yes. The two primary ways of spreading viruses are e-mail attachments and newsgroup binaries. You've heard it before, but it's the best advice: if you receive an e-mail attachment from a stranger, don't open it. If it's from a friend, make sure you know what it is first, and that it hasn't been sent on by half the world beforehand. If it ends with .exe, be even more suspicious. If you're a Mac owner, be smug – there are far fewer Mac viruses, but still be careful. If it's a Word or Excel macro (this applies to PC and Mac users), don't go anywhere near it. If you don't want to get viruses from newsgroups, the rule is simple: never download any binaries (attached files, which may be programs, sounds, pictures, anything). And install some good antivirus software before you do anything.

☞ *What are cookies and what do they say about me?*

If you've ever shopped at a site such as *www.amazon.co.uk* more than once and have found yourself being greeted with a cheery 'Hi, Dave Green, welcome back!', this is due in part to things called cookies. These are little scraps of data which a website saves to your computer so that it can look for them the next time you visit. All it can actually do is register what browser you're using and boring things like that, as a kind of ID number, but if you've entered other details, such as your name and e-mail address, into a database on the site, then that information can be associated with that cookie by the database … and they know who you are. Access the same site from another computer, however, and they won't know you from Eve. If you're paranoid, cookies might seem a threat, but all they really do is mark whether you've been to a particular site before – and what have you got to hide? If you like, you can go to the options/preferences in your browser and refuse to accept cookies, although some sites will not work properly if you do.

☞ *Can my personal data be copied?*

Any data which appears as text onscreen can, of course, be saved and copied, and there have been tales of rogue recruitment sites doing just that: grabbing lists of jobhunters or job vacancies from one site and then listing them on their own. But it's not big and it's not clever, as lawyer John Warchus of Shadbolt & Co explains: 'There is a copyright issue, and also database rights. Database rights are not quite as strong as copyright but do give some element of protection.'

That's protection for the site which has been 'robbed', of course, but you too have rights: 'The individual would probably have a remedy or claim on the basis that they haven't disclosed their personal details to the other party. So they shouldn't really be posted up – it would be using personal data without authority,' says John Warchus.

The idea could linger in your mind, of course, that data is being freely exchanged between sites, although with any of the main jobsites it's unlikely. However, if you've registered with a dozen sites, the chances are you'll get a few unexpected e-mails (*see* below) from rogue sites or greedy recruitment agencies. John Warchus says of the jobsites: 'They should flag up if they're thinking of sending data to any third party. They should really get your consent. If they don't they could be in breach of the data protection laws.'

So look for the small print: every good site should have some. On *www.monster.co.uk*, for example, you'll find a link to its 'Privacy commitment'. With regard to online CVs, it says: 'We use our best efforts to grant access to this database only to paying recruiters, hiring managers, headhunters, and human resource professionals …' Anyone who contacts you, in other words, should be a legitimate user of the site – and remember that you can always elect not to give your e-mail address to a site, or in some cases can suppress it until your permission has been given to pass it on.

👉 *Am I being spied on by my employer?*

It's happening more and more, but unless your employer has a clear IT policy warning of this, you could have a right to defend your privacy. Take a look at Chapter 9 for more on the issue of surfing at work.

👉 *Am I going to be inundated with e-mails I didn't solicit?*

Hopefully not, although you should again always read the small print if you're entering your e-mail address into a form. There's more on the issue of 'spam' and unwanted e-mail in Chapter 9.

—— Real-time **conversation** ——

These forms of communication are all, in a sense, still quite passive: you can send a message and receive a reply, but there's no guarantee if and when that reply will come. In the case of web forums and newsgroups, you have to look for a reply, too.

Needless to say, a more dynamic alternative is also available: the chatroom.[23] This again comes in web and non-web manifestations. Non-web chat is usually known as IRC (internet relay chat). This involves setting up dedicated software and using specialised commands to communicate with other users through your terminal. There are 'channels' dedicated to particular discussions, a bit like the old channels that CB radios used, except that there's no limit to how many there are, and they are often subject-based in a way that CB never was. You can look up chat channels at *www.liszt.com/chat*. The majority are not as specifically themed as the other forms of communication we've been looking at. Want to know more about IRC or other forms of direct communication such as AOL instant messaging? You can read up at *www.chatting.about.com*.

For your purposes, web-based chat will probably offer more than enough of interest, and given that internet connections have become so much faster and more reliable than when IRC was born, there's less of an incentive to avoid the web anyway.

23 What about internet telephony? **page 133.**

So what does 'chat' mean exactly in the internet context? A chatroom is simply a dedicated bit of cyberspace where you can type messages which can be seen and read instantly by other people sharing the same 'space'. Within this framework, just as you could in a real room, it's also possible to exchange messages privately with someone, as if you were whispering to them alone. This means that you could envisage an internet equivalent of the milkround where you could ask a company representative a general question, the answer to which your fellows or rivals might be interested in, and then take that rep aside to explain why they should give you in particular a job on the spot – although employers don't seem to have wised up to this idea just yet.

Some of the jobsites are already hosting their own chatrooms, and it's well worth watching out for them. Sometimes a particular expert will be on hand for a specific after-noon, say. You could then join in on that day and 'meet' them 'directly'. Try *www.chat.careerpath.com* or *www.exp.com*.

_____ A few words **about chat** _____

Web-based chatrooms often work slightly more slowly than non-web ones, as they have to load up special programs (often in Java) in your browser, but they are also often much easier to use. And the general watchwords are the same in both cases:

☞ be brief and to the point;

☞ let other people finish before you type a reply;

☞ don't be rude or aggressive;

☞ don't paste in huge amounts of text;

☞ don't try to dominate a group discussion – let everyone have their say.

Communicating in this way is a strange feeling at first. If you mistype, your audience can see (if you've pressed return too quickly and only then realised your mistake). But there's no substitute for real-time communication and real human beings at both ends of it. Give it a go.

_____ Three clicks **away** _____

At Monster, the philosophy is that you are only three clicks away from the job you want. It really can be true, not just at Monster, but anywhere. Well, it may not always be three clicks, but the point is that the internet thrives, and indeed survives, on communication and exchange. The different ways of meeting people discussed in this chapter might not always seem an obvious way of getting a job as such, but they can introduce you to people who can help.

This might just form part of a wider research exercise, defining your goals or deciding whether your dream career really is the right thing for you. There are other ways of addressing that question, but talking to people on the spot, whether it's by phone, in person, through e-mail or in an online forum, can only help.[24]

If you make yourself known in the right places, you're sure to meet the right people. One of the persistent problems in the world of employment is that people-you-know are often more useful than what-you-know. The internet can help you know more to start with, and find the right people to show what you know. There are no guarantees, but if you get talking with the people in the right way, without bombarding anyone with begging letters, you might even get to hear of a job that's not being advertised. If you can befriend an expert in a large company, they might be able to tell you about internal vacancies, for example. Anything's possible.

So if opportunity knocks as you follow trains of thought and pathways of information on the internet, don't be afraid to answer.

_____ Time for **a quick half** _____

If you've read through the first half of this book, you should feel confident that you can:

- ☞ search for job vacancies online;
- ☞ set up agents to automate that search;
- ☞ build an online CV;
- ☞ research different markets;
- ☞ get the lowdown on particular organisations;

24 How do I know I'm looking for the right kind of job? **page 115.**

☞ refine search engine enquiries to get meaningful results;

☞ track down useful e-mail addresses;

☞ find specialised websites;

☞ join in with online discussions.

So now it's time to complete the circuit.

_____ A brush **with fame** _____

This chapter's exercise is a little more fun but will give you the chance to get used to the feel of internet chat sessions. Point your browser to *www.bbc.co.uk/livechat* and you'll see a list of chat sessions associated with various TV programmes. There are often celebrities appearing online for a session, or there may be a chance to enter into a discussion with the presenter of a documentary. Have a go.

_____

CHAPTER SIX

Applying yourself

Presentation is the **key to success**

We all want a job that stimulates us, invites us to use our full potential, and rewards us mentally, emotionally and financially

Given the number of opportunities that are claimed to be available on the internet, it's easy to lose your way in the throng. Armed with this guide, you'll have learned a lot of valuable skills by now, some of which were listed at the end of the last chapter. If you have been pursuing a new job through the internet seriously, you've probably come across some opportunities that you'd actually like to consider.

However, if you haven't found any suitable opportunities yet, stop and think what it might mean. First of all, it almost certainly does not mean that you are actually doing anything *wrong*, rather that you could be doing some things *better*. You may be unlucky, too: there may simply not be enough opportunities out there in your field at the moment, and/or it may be an area of employment where the internet has genuinely not become a prime means of recruiting. Whatever else happens, you can be sure that will change very soon.

If you think the opportunities really are there, but you're just not getting to them, rethink your strategy and come at the problem again from various angles – follow the 'hyperlinks' for appropriate tips.

☞ Are your search agents optimised for success, or did you put in a few hasty keywords assuming that would do?[1]

☞ Did you really take time and trouble over your online CV? Don't just cut and paste an old one: make a new one and make it work.[2]

☞ Don't just use the big jobsites: use niche sites,[3] read up on the employers. And use the search engines with precision.[4]

☞ Get to know people, make connections, establish contacts, ask questions.[5]

_____ The long and **the short of it** _____

The availability of jobs often appears to be overwhelming. Some of them seem attractive, but you know it's got to be right or it just won't work for you – and you won't work for it. Even if you clap eyes on your dream job very quickly, love at first sight can be a one-sided business: having found what you are looking for you have to convince the employer to give you the job.

In some fields, this can happen very quickly; we've all heard tales of hire 'em and fire 'em organisations, particularly in the City, although they seem to be less common these days. Few people are even looking for a job for life now, but we all want a job that stimulates us, invites us to use our full potential, and rewards us mentally, emotionally and financially. And even if we're only intending to stay in it for three years, the culture is such today that it's not too much to expect all of those things on such a relatively short-lived basis.

According to research by *www.workthing.com*, at the time of writing 3 million internet users in work are likely to change jobs in the next six months – that's a lot of people wanting to be on the move, and employers have no choice but to catch up with them and be more flexible.[6]

As often as not, the process of getting hitched to your dream job does not happen overnight, however, and there may well be several stages you will have to go through. The second half of this book will take you through them, including:

1 How can I get the results I want from search agents? **pages 36–37.**
2 How should I approach an online CV? **page 40, page 103.**
3 How do I find a niche recruitment site? **page 61.**
4 Tell me about advanced search techniques, **page 22.**
5 How can I get in touch with different experts? **Chapters 2, 4 and 5.**
6 I want to be so flexible I don't have to go out to work. What can I do? **page 65, page 130.**

☞ online applications

☞ tools and tests for evaluating your suitability

☞ interviews – in person and at a distance.

Only you can assess the demand for the kind of skills you have, with the help of a careers adviser of some kind, perhaps. What we're saying throughout this book is that the internet can be one such adviser. It doesn't have to be the only one, but it can definitely bring you in touch with a lot of useful advice you've never been given before (as well as some that you've seen all too often, which is why learning to be selective as you surf is one of the most valuable skills of all).

If you're sticking with your current career, you'll probably know what's going on in that field, but you can still make good use of the net to bring the news straight to your desktop.[7] If you're changing career, the net can provide huge resources both in terms of how to go about making the change and for educating yourself in new arenas.[8] The internet, in other words, brings things to you like a faithful dog delivering the slippers. But what it can't do is actually get you the job. That's up to you, and here it's how you use the internet as a medium of communication that becomes important.

> **"While I was travelling in New Delhi, a friend e-mailed me to tell me about a job, so I went to the website, *www.rasnet.co.uk* (for Civil Service jobs), downloaded the PDF application forms and printed them out. I then found out it was cheaper to e-mail them back than fax them, so I filled them in, scanned them back into a computer in Kathmandu and sent them as an attachment!"**
>
> Andrew Akleman, international politics graduate and internet jobhunter

First **contact**

One thing is certain: you can't get a job without applying for it. Well, that's not strictly true – if you've really made some good contacts, particularly with potential employers but maybe with agencies too, you might find that jobs can just come your way unbidden.

7 How do I get the news in a particular sector? **pages 20–21, page 138.**
8 Can I use the net to learn new skills? **pages 147–150.**

But in all probability, you'll have seen a few likely suspects in your search results, and now you have to turn your mind to applying for them. As ever, the bigger jobsites tend to make this pretty easy.

Traditionally, applying for a job – which you'd probably seen in a newspaper ad – meant spending your valuable time (not to mention your money on expensive stationery, perhaps) labouring at covering letters and CVs, wearing out your inkjet cartridges. That can now be a thing of the past (although not necessarily).

Many employers still do not trust the internet as a medium, either for security reasons or plain old Luddism. They may feel that they cannot truly know what you're about from the uniform look of an e-mail, say.[9] But they'd be wrong, and any medium, however limited its range of formal expression, can be used to express yourself well and wisely.

In general, jobsites on the internet will present you with a collection of results that correspond to your search criteria, and you will then be able to click on a link under each to read more comprehensive information; sometimes the site will present as much information about the vacancy as is available at this first stage. When you see the full details, you may well have the option of reading a 'company profile',[10] plus there'll be a button saying something like 'Apply now' or 'Apply online'. On clicking this you are likely to be presented with one of the following scenarios:

👉 the link will open up your e-mail program and invite you to send a message to the person whose e-mail address has been put in for you already;

👉 a form will appear into which you can type a 'covering letter' and perhaps paste or attach a CV;

👉 the site will invite you to send the company a CV you have already created and stored.

Cover **yourself**

Covering letter plus CV (sometimes both replaced by an application form) has long been the standard approach to applying for a job. At the moment, online recruitment tends to work very much to the same model, simply translating these elements to work across the

9 Is this putting graphologists out of business? **pages 113–114.**
10 What are company profiles? **page 24.**

web or via e-mail rather than good old snail mail. As online recruitment truly becomes part of everyday life for everyone, this may well change, and better, more effective ways of doing things might become the norm: recording a brief video portfolio of yourself and your achievements, for example.[11] For now, though, you're basically stuck with the old model, and a lot of the traditional advice dispensed in this direction will still apply.

_____ Covering letters – **the essential points** _____

Grammar: polite and well-formed letters work wonders. You may use the first person, but try to avoid starting every paragraph with 'I' and 'my' – it makes you look self-centred. Recruiters want to know that you have your mind on what they need, not what you want.

Open and shut: start with a very brief opening paragraph that expresses your interest in a position that matches your skills and perhaps includes a request for further detail. Close with an extremely brief paragraph that thanks them for their time and perhaps hints that you are available to talk things over.

Demands: unless you are the only candidate on earth who can do that job, _never_ make demands or conditions of any kind – the place for that is when they want to appoint you, way down the line after several interview stages. Mention your salary _if they ask_, but otherwise leave it out. Salary levels are used to define position, but there are better ways for you to position yourself (role, vision, scope, skills, etc).

The big three: to fit one page you probably have room for just three main paragraphs and unless you are in a sector where long statements are the norm (such as teaching), three is about all you can expect anyone to read, especially in e-mail format. A paragraph, in proper grammar, is one main idea surrounded by qualifying phrases.

– **I'm worth considering:** the first of your big three points, after your introduction, is a very rapid summary of your role, level, scope, experience, filtering through only the absolutely relevant highlights of your career.

11 What about interviews by videolink? **pages 130–134.**

> – **I am relevant:** the second big issue is to relate what you can do to what they want, again in general and exciting terms that do not repeat all the detail in your CV (which they will now read if your letter generates curiosity).
>
> – **This is appropriate:** your last major paragraph, before the polite close, is an opportunity to talk about special qualities, what more you could achieve in the right environment, why you are ready for change, and why they could be the right organisation. This is about synergy and timeliness. Don't try to be too specific because your *only objective* here is to arouse their outline interest.
>
> © Steven Holmes and John Peters. This section is licensed for publication by Monster. You can contact them for advice and assistance on *www.cvservices.net*.

Having said that, 'flexibility' has been the great claim for the internet all along, and it applies here, too. E-mail, for example, has acquired a more informal culture around it, and the 'rules of the game' are subtly different – check out the panel opposite.

The first thing to realise when you're composing an online covering letter, whether it's by standard e-mail or through a web-based form (the end results are little different), is that, even more than before, brevity is more than just the soul of wit: it's vital. Think of your own workplace. The chances are that you use e-mail on a regular basis, maybe constantly, depending on your field and how technologically savvy your employers are. How many e-mails do you get a day – two or three, maybe? Or perhaps even two or three dozen? If you've been away on holiday for a week or more, you'll probably know the nightmare of 'information overload' that greets you in your inbox on your return.[12] Think, therefore, what it must be like to be on the receiving end of hundreds of e-mailed job applications.

Applications in this form do not have the opportunity to stand out in the same way as traditional ones do. You cannot choose brightly coloured paper or enclose a £5 note – not that you should do either of these anyway. E-mails can only really stand out by being worth reading, and that almost certainly means by being exceedingly to the point (but not rude, of course). E-mail has its own conventions, too, and you'll probably be laughed at if

12 How do I stem the tide of e-mails? **page 142.**

you were to put your entire address and that of the recipient, say, at the top of your message. In some circumstances, even a 'Dear Sir/Madam' might be more than is needed.

E-mail covering letters – **the netiquette**

☞ *Be brief and to the point*
The unlimited possible length of an e-mail is not a licence to waffle. In the same way that websites should not oblige the reader to scroll down for more than one or two screens, keep your e-mails brief.

☞ *Express yourself*
Many jobsites will automatically put a very basic covering letter into the online application form, but try to rephrase it in your own words. Even if you're not really saying much different ('I would like to apply for the post of Grommet Polisher …'), it shows you're making the effort. An employer receiving endless e-mails where the applicants couldn't even be bothered to write their own covering letter might not be impressed.

☞ *Be serious, but be simple*
Don't be overformal or pompous: there's no need for 'yours sincerely' or whatever. Much more common in the e-mail world is to sign off with 'Best regards', 'With thanks', or something snappy like that. But don't be over-familiar, unless you're applying for a job in California.[13]

☞ *Cut down the original text when using 'Reply'*
If you reply to a message from an employer (ar anyone else for that matter), try not to include the whole of the original message unless it is strictly necessary. There is nothing wrong with cutting it down to the bare bones to remind the sender of what it was all about or to draw attention to a particular point. There's nothing worse than a message that has been passed on round the houses where you can read the e-mail header information automatically added to it every time someone has passed it on to a friend with the

13 Any tips on applying for jobs abroad? **page 64.**

> apparently innocent and brief message 'Check this out, mate' – not that you
> should be sending the latest round of e-mail jokes to a potential employer.
>
> ☞ *Give the right information*
> Your contact information should be part of any CV that you're sending, but
> give a phone number in your covering letter. Don't bother to say what your
> e-mail address is as they'll have that automatically, of course.

There will always remain an element of uncertainty about what tone to adopt, since it depends upon the personality of the person reading your application. And however auto-mated recruitment is becoming, there is a real person reading your words somewhere. Your best guide is probably to think about the kind of field in which you are working or hoping to work. More traditional areas, such as law, are more likely to expect a higher degree of formality in terms of dress, manner and even your prose; conversely, in the world of the internet, you are more likely to be taken seriously if you don't take things too seriously.

But it depends, and if you've never enjoyed writing covering letters and do not feel confident about the tone you should adopt, you can always phone up and speak to a real person. Employers are usually pretty busy, but they also want to hire the right people, and they're unlikely to mind you phoning to show your interest.

The other side **of the fence**

As a jobhunter, you know only too well how many people you can be up against, and if the internet makes applying for jobs easier, numbers are likely to keep increasing. All this represents a great deal of work for the employer, so how are they coping?[14]

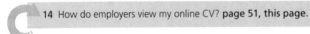

14 How do employers view my online CV? **page 51, this page.**

The human resources (HR) team at Abbey National has been facing as many as 2 500 graduate applications, all within a six-week period every year. They are now using a system called JobSift created by psychometrics experts PSL.[15] JobSift enables the employer to set up tailor-made questionnaires for applicants, which are then analysed for evidence of desired skills and character traits, thus narrowing down the field of applicants which the HR team needs to consider.

Online recruiter Stepstone has signed up to a deal which enables employers using its site to take advantage of the JobSift system. For the employer, this can mean a major financial saving, and as Stepstone's CEO Giles Clarke says: 'While recruiters will be assured that they are getting the best candidate for the job, candidates will know that they are getting the best job for them.'

Form **and content**

So much for the form, but the content is all important, and that's where you're selling yourself. An e-mail covering letter, like any other, includes both necessary and accessory information. In terms of the necessities, you must, unless something obvious dictates that you can omit them, refer to:

- ☞ what the job is;
- ☞ why you're writing (i.e. to apply for it);
- ☞ why you're appropriate for it.

Of course, it's this last section that's the hardest to write and which may well overlap with the 'additional information' aspect. The general principle is to explain very concisely that you have appropriate experience for the job in question, which then gives the employer the opportunity to glean more detail (assuming it's there!) from your CV. But there are always exceptions, and in the fast world of the internet, some employers might call you in on the basis of the covering letter alone. There may come a time when CVs as

15 Tell me more about this kind of testing and selection, **Chapter 7.**

we know them die out and a lot of people will probably heave a big sigh of relief. But it hasn't happened just yet. It's no bad thing to include your phone number in a covering letter: not everyone is as enthusiastic about e-mail as you might be. But the covering letter is not the appropriate place to go into your personal aspirations and obsession with collecting small plastic models of farmyard animals: these niceties are best saved for the interview, which is another business altogether.[16]

_____ Got it **covered** _____

A few watchwords for covering letters in any medium:

☞ don't forget to send one – an unannounced CV risks oblivion;

☞ use it to connect your CV to the vacancy;

☞ be factual and accurate;

☞ be brief, but also be polite;

☞ avoid clichés like 'I want to work with people'.

Look out for sites which let you set up covering letters in advance of specific applications – *www.jobsite.co.uk* and *www.monster.co.uk*, for example, let you write up to four of them for posterity, and you can choose which one goes out with a particular application.[17]

E-mail is a strange medium, in the sense that it allows a great deal of informality and flexibility of expression yet certain standards are still expected. If in doubt, you should probably err on the side of being conservative, and however fluid your mode of expression, you should still take the trouble to put your potted history into grammatical English. Just because your potential employer whacks off a five-word reply all in lower case, with a spelling mistake and a solecism to boot, it is unlikely to impress them if you do the same.

16 Tell me about interviews, **Chapter 8.**
17 Can I set up more than one CV? **pages 41 and 54.**

Passing **references**

Should you include references in your online CV or covering letter? If an online CV form has space for them, then yes; otherwise, no. If an employer wants references, they can always ask you when they get in touch: at this stage it's how you present yourself that matters.

There are important legal issues with references, of course, and it's important to tell your referees you've put their names down.[18] Expert in 'e-law' John Warchus of Shadbolt & Co says: 'There have been some serious cases with regard to references. You obviously can't insist the employer gives a favourable reference but there is a duty of care now on employers when they give a reference to make sure that it's accurate. That would apply to a reference sent by e-mail as much as anything else.'

Developing **attachments**

A lot of these points are pertinent to your CV, too, although you've probably already learned them in Chapter 3. Like most other things you're likely to create online, your CV needs to be:

- concise
- accurate
- targeted to the audience.

If you've already created an online CV, all well and good, but it is perfectly possible with many jobsites to have got as far as the application stage without having been encouraged to think about your CV at all. It's easy to be misled into thinking you can knock one off quickly at the last minute before clicking 'Submit' – but it isn't recommended.

Some sites almost make it too easy to apply. In the case of Monster, you'll have had to create an online CV beforehand in order to send a full application online; if you've already done this, one click will send your CV (without a specific covering letter). If

18 What other legal issues should I know about? **page 87, pages 140 and 152.**

you've created more than one carefully crafted CV, therefore, it's particularly important to select the right one before you fire it off.

Monster provides an e-mail contact for the employer, too: this means that even if you haven't taken the trouble to build a proper online CV (and you are advised to: employers using a site that works like this will of course expect to hear from applicants in this way, if they haven't already found you for themselves[19]), you can still send a message. You could use this to enquire for more details about the job, or simply to send an e-mail covering letter with your own-design CV attached.

The word 'attachments' conceals a minefield of its own. Being able to send any kind of file with an e-mail message is a powerful tool, but also one widely open to abuse. It's also one of the primary ways in which viruses are spread, so employers need to know what they're getting is harmless, just as you do.[20]

_____ All about **file formats** _____

What format should you send attachments in? Here are the most common.

- ☞ **Plain text**, or **ASCII**: you are guaranteed that anyone who gets this will be able to read it, but what they won't see is anything you've put into bold, italics or a particular font, etc.

- ☞ **RTF**: this stands for Rich Text Format, and is supposed to be an agreed standard, similar to plain text but allowing you to use emphasis such as bold and italic. However, not all RTFs are exactly the same, and it is probably best avoided.

- ☞ **Word**: most companies use Microsoft Word as their chief word-processing software (or Office, of which it forms a part). There are many different versions of Word, however, so unless you're sure that they've got the latest version, you could save back as Word 6.0/95 to be on the safe side. Mac users should do the same: this version is less prone to translation problems, bearing in mind that most employers also use PCs.

19 Tell me about how employers use jobsites, **pages 49–50.**
20 What do I need to know about viruses? **page 86.**

Another format every web user should know about is **PDF**, although it's unlikely you'll use this for a CV or letter. PDF (Portable Document Format) was created by Adobe to offer a standard format which can be used for publishing across a variety of media: in other words, it looks the same on paper as it does on the web. You'll often find information files in PDF, particularly on government sites, as it's very economical with server space. To open PDFs, you need the free Acrobat Reader program – if it's not already installed as a plug-in in your browser (check the options or preferences menu for plug-ins or 'helpers'), you can download it from *www.adobe.com*.

If in doubt, send your CV or whatever as a Word file and as plain text (i.e. as two attachments in the same document, and name the file **jsmith.doc** and **jsmith.txt** or similar to make it clear which is which). Don't just call it 'CV', as they won't know whose it is.

Don't send pictures unless specifically requested: they often take up too much memory and therefore too much telephone time or bandwidth to download. In general, try to avoid sending any attachments that are bigger than 200K, and even this would be unlikely as an average CV in Word format will be less than 50K in size.

If you're attaching your CV, the golden rule is that you should keep it as focused, accurate and concise as if you'd created it in an online CV builder or anywhere else. There is a strong temptation with attachments to go into too much detail, just because you can: but don't. The general principle of keeping your CV to two pages, or preferably to one, holds here as much as ever. If you've already created a paper CV in a program such as Microsoft Word, you can probably send that and all will be well, but read the tips here. There are many formats which employers might not be able to open, and they will probably ignore them rather than make the effort to learn about them.

Again, although fancy fonts and so on are suddenly an option again, don't bother. What an employer really wants to see, onscreen and off, is a neat and simply presented package, where the following information can be found instantly:

☞ who you are;

☞ how to contact you;

☞ what you're doing now.

If they like what they see, they can read on to find:

☞ who you'd like to be;

☞ what you've done before;

☞ what you can bring to the job.

If they like that too, you're well on the way.

> **"Sending an effective, well-targeted CV presents the same problems in hard copy or online. In either case initial perusal by an employer is likely to last less than one minute unless something attracts their attention. A poorly presented, badly organised CV will end up in a wastepaper basket or a PC recycle bin. Think carefully about what you are applying for, and who you are applying to. Common mistakes are poor attention to relevant dates with gaps in the employment history, a lack of focus on the most relevant parts of employment history, and a tendency to give lists of personal strengths and qualities without evidencing these. Current fashion in CVs favours short sentences and a great emphasis on personal qualities and skills."**
>
> Sue Hodgson, independent career consultant

_____ To follow **or not to follow** _____

Having fired off your covering letter and/or CV by e-mail or across the web, what happens next? Ideally, of course, they'll call you and offer you the job the next day – after all, e-mail allows for a much faster response than the post. Next best, they'll call you in for an interview, or not in at all, perhaps, as there are now other ways of conducting interviews.[21]

What we all know happens far more often than either of these is nothing. It's common for employers, inconsiderate as it is, to take weeks to respond to postal applications, and just because they *could* respond to an e-mail immediately doesn't mean they *will*. The question is: should you stalk your application? In other words, when is it appropriate to follow up? Perhaps this question is best dealt with by rephrasing it altogether: not *when* but *how*. If you've still not heard anything after a couple of weeks, it seems fair enough that you should get in touch again and enquire as to the status of your application. Again, you're only showing your interest.

The fact that e-mails can be easily ignored is perhaps a good thing as well as a bad one: if an employer really doesn't want to know, they don't have to, so you perhaps might feel less compunction in firing off a message to solicit the whereabouts of your hopes than you would with conventional means (as long as you don't start 'flaming' them). As ever, the main point is to observe the conventions: be brief. A one-sentence enquiry, polite of course, might well be enough.

> **“It's a humbling experience to be turned down for interview when you may feel you are perfect for the job. But at the same time, sometimes jobhunters forget that for every ad we place we may receive over 200 replies and in most cases only one candidate will be offered the job. I firmly believe, however, that it does us good as search and selection consultants to see things from the jobhunter's point of view.”**
>
> Beth Cauldwell, TMP Worldwide

The speed and simplicity of e-mail can also make it all too easy to send glib and uncaring messages, and if you receive a curt one-liner rejecting your application, it is not going to brighten your day. But you can still send another message, politely enquiring why your application was turned down, and maybe they'll be more forthcoming. And don't forget, e-mail is also easily forgotten.

If you get the thumbs down from one opportunity, you've probably got others lined up: that's the joy of internet recruitment. You can now do what Mother Nature does if

21 Such as? **pages 129–134.**

necessary: send out lots of tadpoles, in the hope that at least some of them turn into handsome frogs.[22]

_____ Cover **pin-ups** _____

As a useful exercise, try writing two or three different covering letters: if you've set up more than one online CV already, tailor them to these in particular. If you're using a site such as GoJobsite.co.uk or monster.co.uk, you could then upload these letters in readiness; otherwise just keep them on your PC for use when one of your CVs gets a bite from an employer.

22 What does the law say about job offers by e-mail? **page 134.**

CHAPTER SEVEN

Testing times

Prepare yourself **for scrutiny**

No decent employer is going to use psychometric testing as their only decision-making tool for whether they should take you on or not

f your line has got a nibble, there's still a knack to landing the catch – and some fish are more slippery than others …

As we've seen, the length of the whole contact-to-contract process can vary a great deal, and while some employers simply want to fill seats fast, others are going to put you through the mill. Once again, the internet can help you be prepared for whatever they might throw at you.

You want a fulfilling and stimulating job for perhaps a few years before you move on to another, and it's now possible. The other side of the coin, your part of the contract as it were, is that the employer needs to know that during those few years you are going to be a valuable part of the system: efficient, effective – and able to get on with your colleagues. This is where evaluation comes in.

Long before we all started turning to glossy magazines to find out 'what we really want from life', people had a fascination with knowing what they know and what sort of person it makes them, and comparing it with others. Psychometric testing and evaluation, although in many ways a modern obsession, has a long history in the sciences of the mind. Today we may be thankful at least that a potential employer is not going to feel the bumps on our head or look for signs of black bile. They're still searching for bumps of a sort, though: various forms of evaluation are widespread throughout the employment world, and they're looking for both your strengths and your weaknesses. This chapter will look at how such instruments are appearing online, and how you can pre-empt the over-inquisitive employer.

Evaluation **evaluated**

Terms such as 'psychometric testing' and 'aptitude assessment' cover a wide field of assessment tools, so it's worth surveying the different types of test that are around and, more importantly, what they're testing.

There's something of a problem of definition to begin with, as terms such as 'ability' and 'aptitude' are often used confusedly, whether it's to mean the same thing or something subtly different. Consider instead what sort of things tests of all kinds can be used to assess:

☞ the skills you have: literacy, numeracy, spatial and abstract reasoning, manual dexterity, and your ability to solve problems of all these kinds;

☞ the potential skills that may be latent within you: you might know you are numerate and logical, for example, but not that you'd be a good computer programmer;

☞ the way you relate to your work;

☞ the way you relate to other people.

The last two might well be used in a specific way, i.e. with regard to the job you're applying for and the kind of team you might be working in, but also in a more general sense to get a feel of who you are, what you aspire to – vague, nebulous things that you probably went to India for a year to find out and still aren't sure of.

Psychology has always had to be a slightly defensive science, not always taken seriously by its gritty cousins in the world of physics and chemistry, for example. This has perhaps contributed to a certain compensatory overconfidence in models of the mind, and the wide variety of testing methods that have grown out of them. Each has its own patch to defend. Nevertheless, certain tools have emerged as the most popular with employers, and they must be getting something right. What's important to remember is that no decent employer is going to use psychometric testing as their only decision-making tool for whether they should take you on or not. Your application has already contributed to that process, and the interview remains a major factor, when the dynamics of real people communicating with each other come into play.

It's also important to listen to what a test might be telling you: if you have answered every question as honestly as you can, it is probably telling you reasonably accurate things about yourself, some of which you might not necessarily want to acknowledge. Be open-minded, and you can improve your skills wisely. Many of the tests an employer uses – unless they are analysing specific skills such as logical reasoning – do not have 'right answers': they are used simply to create a picture of who you are and how you might react in certain situations. This information might be a useful revelation to you as much as to anyone else.

There's a good summary of some of the issues involved, especially any worries you might have, at *www.psychoassess.bizland.com/questions.html*.

_____ Popular **methods** _____

One of the most well known and most popular methods is the Myers-Briggs Type Indicator (MBTI) method of 'personality assessment', often just known as Myers-Briggs.

The Myers-Briggs test was established by Isabel Briggs Myers and her mother Katherine Cook Briggs in the 1920s and developed until it reached its present form in the 1960s and 1970s. It evolved from the work on psychological types by Carl Jung, who gave us the words 'introvert' and 'extrovert'. Myers and Briggs expanded Jung's thinking, feeling, sensate and intuitive personality types into 16 different types. Each consists of four elements in combination:

☞ introverted or extroverted;

☞ sensing or intuitive;

☞ thinking or feeling;

☞ perceiving or judging.

The idea of the first of these is that everybody is either orientated to the world outside them or to the inner world of themselves. The second distinction relates to how you pay attention to the world around you; the third to how you make decisions; and the fourth to how you lead your life – chaotically or well organised, for example.

An obvious drawback of this framework is that many of us seem to fall halfway between the apparent poles, assuming you agree that they are meaningful opposites to start with. Where boundaries are drawn is always going to be a moot point, but Myers-Briggs does at least have the weight of use behind it – even the Church uses Myers-Briggs methods as part of some of its training courses, and there are rumours that it might test applicants in this way. It's all very well to get the call, but the hierarchy needs to know whether you can take the flak. Next time your friends come back from a management training course asking if you think they're too judgemental, you'll know why.

If your curiosity has already been piqued and you'd like to know more about which type you are (abbreviated to four letters, e.g. ESFP: Extrovert Sensate Feeling Perceiver), there are huge amounts of resources on the net about this sort of thing, and there are even web communities devoted to people who belong to a particular category. Check out *www.mbtypeguide.com/Type* for links to some of them. Of course, there are plenty of resources for people into astrology on the net, too …

———— Emotional **intelligence** ————

Myers-Briggs is far from the only popular means of assessing personality and/or skills, and new methodologies are sprouting up all the time. We've all heard of IQ, or 'intelligence quotient', a term which was adopted by US psychologist Lewis Terman in 1915 and popularised in this country, particularly by behavioural psychologist Hans Eysenck. It has become synonymous with a certain kind of assessment revolving primarily around the solving of various logic problems, expressed through literacy, numeracy, abstract and spacial reasoning puzzles.

Although people are often delighted to hear they have a high IQ (membership of Mensa, for example, is conditional on passing various tests like this and establishing an IQ in the top 2 per cent), it does not mean that they are instantly qualified to run the country, and employers have become increasingly sceptical of IQ as a means of assessing people's actual *ability*.

Various theories have developed in reaction to the narrow-mindedness of IQ testing in recent years. One of the most successful is known as 'emotional intelligence'. Its creator, American psychologist Daniel Goleman, is the author of *Emotional Intelligence* (1995) and *Working with Emotional Intelligence* (1998), which have become bestsellers (both published by Bloomsbury). The core of emotional intelligence is awareness of oneself and others. In Goleman's words: 'It is the capacity for recognizing our own feelings and those of others for motivating ourselves, and for managing emotions well in ourselves and in our relationships' (1998).

The theory is that emotionally intelligent employees will help create a business which is more:

- ☞ collaborative
- ☞ flexible
- ☞ resilient
- ☞ innovative.

Your 'EQ', as it were, is intended to complement your IQ, and the basic principle is that however intelligent you are in formal terms, it is how you apply that intelligence, how you express yourself and your abilities emotionally that will ultimately determine your success. You might be a genius, but if you can't relate to other people successfully, particularly in the workplace, you might as well stay in your garret and eat baked beans all day.

Emotional intelligence is being taken seriously by employers. The Hay Group, a major player in recruitment, has even developed a special emotional intelligence unit, which you can learn more of at *http://ei.haygroup.com*.

Write **for the job**

Another form of character analysis that has been popular with employers is graphology, hence the number of newspaper job ads that ask for a handwritten covering letter. Of course, e-mails and online testing are hardly compatible with this. So is graphology threatened by the internet?

'No,' says Margaret White, a founding member of the British Institute of Graphologists. 'There will always be new fads and fancies for the recruitment agencies and some companies to try, but once a company is happy with their consultant graphologist they usually stay with them. Graphology is being used more and more in the UK as an objective and cost-effective tool in selecting personnel and troubleshooting internal staff problems.'

Time will tell, of course, but for now it's still quite likely that an employer will want to see your scrawl. Margaret White offers some tips to stop the nerves shaking the pen:

☞ accept graphology as one of the most objective, accurate and fair methods of assessing character and working qualities;

☞ always insist that you are given an unruled piece of paper on which to write and use either a Biro or fountain pen for preference. Never use a pencil or cheap felt-tipped pen;

☞ be assured that a professional graphologist will write an assessment which is helpful both to the author and to the employer.

Charging **the batteries**

Another tool used widely, for helping people to identify their right career path or vocation, particularly in the US but also over here, is the strong interest inventory or SII. This is used to identify general interests, jobs and recreations that appeal to you, and your likes and dislikes. In other words, it focuses not on what you can necessarily do but on what you want. Often that's the hardest thing to work out. Other 'interest inventories' you might come across are KUDOS and Adult Directions. Go to *www.careerzone-uk.com* and you can take an SII test online in about half an hour.

Another popular testing route employs a combination of SII and MBTI to cover more ground: what you want, and how well you're likely to do whatever it is you want. A third method you might come across is known as FIRO-B – fundamental interpersonal relations orientation-behaviour. Unpack the impenetrable acronym and what it means is assessing your behaviour in the workplace and how what you might work in tandem or in conflict with other people around you.

The fact that each test tends to assess only one aspect of you as a working person is not lost on employers, of course, and increasingly they are combining tests to produce 'batteries' of assessment tools which poke and prod your personal capital from all manner of angles. One such is the Morrisby profile, a very detailed test which takes more than three hours to complete. This will take into account your interests, your abilities and your personality: again, what you want, what you're capable of doing, and how well you're likely to do it.

The best **of the tests**

Here are just some of the psychometric tests in use by employers:

☞ **MBTI** – 16 personality types analysed.

☞ **Insight** – often used in the public sector to measure leadership.

☞ **OPQ** – similar to the test in the exercise at the end of this chapter.

☞ **Omega** – measures motivation and competency.

☞ **PA Preference Inventory** – assesses your preferred way of working.

☞ **Watson-Glaser** – intellectual problem-solving analysed.

☞ **16-PF** – matches personality types to particular jobs.

☞ **DMT** – assesses your emotional development.

☞ **FIRO-B** – behaviour in the workplace.

☞ **Belbin** – used to assess team-playing skills.

Know **thyself**

'Know thyself' was the great buzz-phrase of many an ancient Greek philosopher, most notably Socrates. Your aim is to find out about yourself with respect to improving your career prospects, but even if you don't like what you discover, it should not make you turn to the hemlock.

Many employers in this country use some form of assessment in the recruitment process. Some, such as the Civil Service, have even run them online. You might get lucky and find that you slip through the net and straight into a nice new swivel chair, but don't count on it. As always, it's best to be prepared, and that's where the net comes in.

——— Testy **responses** ———

Testing is not exactly popular with jobhunters, and there is in fact a downward trend in its use by employers. In the US for example, one poll (*source:* AMA) found that among 2 133 firms, the number using psychometrics had fallen from 52 per cent in 1998 to 33 per cent two years later. If too many candidates refuse, then employers are losing potentially good applicants, so unless the internet makes them more user-friendly for everyone and improves their image, you may find that this discussion is only of historical interest.

There are other important issues here, too. A few years ago the public services union Unison called for a ban on the use of psychometric tests in job interviews on the basis that they were found to discriminate against candidates in some ethnic minorities. An employer turning down a foreign applicant on the basis of a hesitant style of writing, say, could also be found to have discriminated. These are good reasons for employers to abandon testing, although for now it remains an issue you should consider, if only for your own self-assessment.

It's well worth looking up some of the top tests online and taking them before you ever get to the application stage. After all, it's all very well applying for jobs that appeal to you, but are they really right for you? Some sites understandably charge for complete testing services, and you will generally only find samplers or cut-down versions of the big-name tests on the web. With the caveat that these are going to be of limited use, it's still worth checking them out. There's a good summary of various psychometric resources at *www.psychology.about.com*.

The *Financial Times* website has a Career Advisor (sic) channel, too, which links to two different kinds of tests you can take online: go to *http://career.ft.com/careers*.[1] One of these offers a brief outline of your 'emotional intelligence' and the other invites you to assess your 'personal values'.

However well you might think you know yourself, there is inevitably always more to learn, and even the mere act of taking one of these tests, with the kind of questions they

---

1 Tell me more about filling in forms on the web, **page 39.**

prompt you to consider, could be considered a useful exercise. Doing a few online tests could also give you ideas about:

☞ careers you haven't considered before;

☞ ways to enjoy yourself more, both at work and away from it;

☞ things to ask at an interview.

The value of the internet as your personal career adviser is always going to be in direct proportion to your willingness to let it stimulate new ideas.

Not every online test you'll come across is serious, of course, and there are a lot of entertaining tests and quizzes which it's easy to be waylaid by. A huge variety of these can be found at *www.emode.com,* for example: here you can find out what breed of dog you are, or whether you have all the hallmarks of an A-grade slacker. These could hardly be said to help in finding out useful things about yourself, but you've got to have *some* fun.

_____ The real **thing** _____

If you've put yourself through your paces on the net beforehand, the threat of real testing by a real employer should be much less daunting. The best way to approach any kind of testing is with an open mind and the hope of actually enjoying yourself. People fill in daft magazine questionnaires for fun and little expectation of enlightenment; in this case, you are doing the same sort of thing, but with the prospect of learning something useful.

Whatever type of testing you are being called in for, and of course you may not be told precisely, there are various watchwords you should bear in mind:

☞ be calm

☞ be open-minded

☞ be truthful

☞ be considered

☞ be yourself.

Above all, be yourself. Anyone who is reasonably observant will probably spot that the way questions are worded in a typical psychometric test invites certain responses from certain kinds of people. Don't try to be someone you aren't.

A similarly observant test analyser will probably be able to spot this, if not now then certainly at interview (unless you're a very accomplished liar, and that is not what this book is intended to teach you), and corny as it sounds, 'you're only cheating yourself'. There's really no point in trying to beat the system to get a job if it isn't really the right job for you and that, after all, is what these tests are about.

Some tests aim to take this natural tendency to assess the assessment into account anyway and are pretty successful at it: when your author was at school he joined in a facetious competition to see who could get 'priest' as the advised career when the class was given a career assessment profile to complete, but nobody got lucky, and it was probably just as well. In fact, those who tried largely ended up with 'author' or 'journalist'. Ah well.

At the other end of the spectrum of possible responses to psychometric testing, it's important not to be intimidated, nor indeed to be afraid of showing an interest in its mechanisms. Not all employers will be keen to share the results of their assessment of you, but there's no harm in asking; in fact, it's your right. Graphologist Margaret White points out: 'Most ethical employers, recruiters and/or vocation counsellors will discuss the assessment with the candidate. And employment law now states that a candidate or employee must be given access to the assessment upon request.'

But even if you don't get the job, whatever tests you've been put through ought to reveal useful pointers to other possibilities and help you find a position elsewhere. Interpreting the results may require more expert guidance, however; although knowing you're perceptive and intuitive might offer a vague sense of direction, knowing how to read properly the results of a test like the MBTI requires skill and training. This is where a good recruitment consultant or careers adviser can still play a useful role, and as yet such one-to-one opportunities are limited on the internet, particularly if what you're discussing is fundamentally personal and you do not want to air your dirty habits in full view of the world on a discussion forum.[2]

2 How do discussion forums work? **page 74.**

> **❝People usually require help in decision making, career planning and self presentation, and will still turn to a person for much of this support. Careers and employment information research, however, lends itself very well to the internet, allowing people access to company information, journals and reference material such as trade directories, year books and information specific to individual companies.❞**
>
> Sue Hodgson, independent career consultant

It also bears repeating that you should not be disheartened by what you learn: if your aptitudes are inclined towards market gardening rather than astrophysics, it doesn't mean there aren't ways and means to fulfil what you're interested in as much as what you're capable of. Again, this is where professional advice is invaluable.

The final point is that however much testing your prospective employer may put you through, it's only half the picture. It's like listening to the radio: you form an image of the presenter in your mind based on their voice, the things they say and so on, but you still wouldn't be able to draw them accurately unless you're psychic, which seems to be a talent left unanalysed by most tests you'll come across. Until you actually see someone, you can't really know what they're like. And that's where interviews come in.

———— The internet **is your kingdom** ————

One apparently fun-but-frivolous test on the net is worth trying out. Check out *www.kingdomality.com* and you will find a simple eight-question test that offers to reveal what your role in society would have been in medieval times. Although there's not much to the test and of course your opportunities of being, say, a 'benevolent ruler' are likely to be limited, this test is quite effective at producing a broad-brush picture of your strengths and weaknesses. It's also hosted by a serious recruitment organisation called Career Management International (*www.cmi-lmi.com*).

CHAPTER EIGHT

Face to face ...
but maybe apart

The cyberspace approach **to interviewing**

Now there's no reason why you can't seek, apply for, be

tested and be interviewed for a job without meeting a single

person in the flesh

nterviews. Does anyone really like them? 'Just be yourself.' 'It's your chance to show them who you are and what you can do.' Well yes, but it's also your chance to screw up and lose the job, as everyone knows.

The important thing is not to make a mountain out of a medium-sized hill. Of course an interview is a very significant hurdle to cross on your path to career nirvana, but it's also one of many, and if you've got this far, you've crossed most of them already.

In a sense, the interview *per se* is the culmination of a series of smaller, more specific interviews that you might not have even considered yourself as having gone through. If your application has attracted interest – in other words you've been invited in for a test or for an interview – then you've been 'interviewed' already in a way. When your CV lands in the employer's inbox or, poor traditionalist that he or she is, in their pigeonhole, the two minutes or 20 seconds that they devote to reading it is an assessment of precisely who you are (or claim to be) and what you can offer with respect to the company and the position for which you've applied.[1]

---

1 What format should I send it in? **page 104.**

The same goes for psychometric or aptitude testing.[2] In this case your personality or your skills are being assessed on paper, which will probably miss all the subtleties of your manner and the way you communicate, but you could think of it as a type of interview nonetheless. In fact, some employers even call people in for specific 'behavioural interviews', which involve asking you about your experience of different situations and how you handled them.[3]

We all perceive ourselves to have particular strengths and weaknesses, regardless of what the psychometric tests tell you. At school or college, for example, you may have considered yourself good at essays but bad at exams, or vice versa. In just the same way that people used to say 'Oh, I'm no good at exams', they now say 'Oh, I'm no good at interviews', as if the medium of testing were the test itself.

A testing time it may be, but like any medium of communication – and that's exactly what both exams and interviews are – it's really a question of learning the vocabulary and the rules for putting it together. Ultimately, though, it is also what you say that matters, and if you've got this far, they must think you're a viable candidate, and they'd like to hear what you have to say.

The difference now is that there are new ways of meeting your employer in order to say it. Fast and lazy forms of communication like e-mail are inevitably influencing the hiring process – it's not inconceivable that you could even be interviewed by e-mail. More likely, though, is a videoconference interview – you'll find the rules of this latest game in this chapter.

_____ Prepare to **meet your maker** _____

Regardless of whether you meet your prospective bosses in person or in absentia, there are general watchwords for the whole interview arena which have stood the test of time. The vast majority of employers are still relying on the good old face-to-face, sit-down-make-yourself-comfortable affair, and many of the general approaches you are advised to take apply just as much to the new technologies which allow you to avoid the boss's bad breath or wet handshake.

It's easy to let interviews creep up on you, particularly if you are devoting your energies both to applying for new jobs and to holding down the one you've already got. It's

2 What does psychometric testing involve? **page 110.**
3 What method do they use? **page 115.**

easy, in other words, to remember you have an interview on the self-same morning, throw on some clothes, bolt for the door and pretend to yourself that any preparation you need to do can be done in your head on the Tube. What makes it harder to offer good advice is that we all know people who've done just that: crawled out of bed, rushed to the interview at the last minute, lied through their teeth, and got the job. In no way, however, is this a recommendation. And the same person might well have been forced to do exactly the same thing three months later when they were rumbled.

So the message here is, be prepared. If you know you've got an interview coming up, it's really not that hard to spare an hour or two to think about it beforehand. And there are three easy things to remember that will stand you in good stead:

- ☞ think ahead
- ☞ travel light
- ☞ be focused.

'Think ahead' means, of course, think about the job you've applied for and the firm it's part of, and what sort of questions you might be asked in the interview. They'll want to know how well you know them and what to expect, and why you want the job. You might not be sure about it anyway, and that for you could be a reason for going to the interview – to make up your mind. Remember what you are looking for from the job, from salary to responsibility. All the more reason for thinking about it beforehand.

Thinking ahead also means making practical preparations for the interview: getting your 'interview suit' ready, cleaning your shoes or having the infamous jobhunter's hair-cut. Maybe you work in a respectable field already and these are part of your everyday life, but maybe the job you're going for is more flexible and trendy, and everyone's got hair down to their ankles. There's still no harm in thinking about these things, and striking a balance at least.

And thinking ahead means bringing relevant materials with you. If you're a graphic designer, you'd be laughed at without a portfolio under your arm, or a laptop, perhaps. Whatever field you're going for, you are well advised to bring spare copies of your CV. It's surprising how many employers seem to have 'lost' yours before you arrive at the interview – maybe some of them arrive at the last minute and lie through their teeth, too. You're assessing them as well, remember.[4]

---

4 Are there any objective assessments of employers? **page 24.**

You need to look organised: you don't want scraps of paper flapping around. Bring a file, then, with any relevant documents: how to get there, the letters they've sent you, your original covering letter and CV, and anything that might provide at-a-glance evidence of things you've done. But travel light. This means don't carry a great rucksack as if you've just come back from Nepal (even if you have) or anything that's going to be a nuisance. There's nothing worse than arriving at a shiny new office block and wondering where to put your army surplus gear.

But 'travel light' means something more important, too. It means don't bring too many fears, hopes or expectations: just be open-minded, without emotional baggage, and ready to meet people on an intelligent, equal basis for the exchange of ideas, albeit ideas revolving around who you are and what you can bring to the organisation. The point is that you have all the intellectual luggage you need already – that's why they've called you in – so don't burden yourself with anything unnecessary, physically or psychologically.

This will help you 'be focused'. Obviously you need to know something about the job beforehand, and it's in your interests to do a little background research – if you're applying online, make sure you do some research online. There's no harm in phoning the company beforehand, to see an annual report, brochure or other publication, perhaps, or just to clarify a few things with someone on the spot. Or find the company on the internet.[5] Then when you're on the spot, you'll be that much more informed and articulate.

Part of clearing your mind of unnecessary baggage and being focused lies in the secret of knowing how to relax. Naturally you don't want to arrive half asleep, with them thinking you're some kind of space cadet, but a few deep breaths and exercises beforehand, not to mention a good night's sleep, are always more valuable than they seem.

Preparing **for interview**

You are a brand: if you prepared a great application you will now have created an image in the minds of the recruiters. Think about that image and try to live up to or exceed it when you actually meet them. Go as yourself as well – which is the tricky part, because they will be wanting to find out who you really are and how you will react to working conditions.

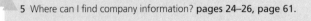

5 Where can I find company information? **pages 24–26, page 61.**

Curiosity: they are going to be scanning your CV and application letter at the interview, picking out the points you mentioned and asking for further detail. It's a good idea to prepare and rehearse the landmarks and key issues so that they come naturally to you when the conversation is flowing. Interviewers warm to candidates who want to know exactly what the role entails, what the company is about and what future plans are. It makes you seem astute and keen, so don't be afraid to respond to their questions with questions of your own.

Give yourself space: don't be rushed, and take a deep breath if you lose balance. It's fine to ask for clarification and it's good to waste a bit of time with warm human narrative and establishing a relationship. If you can't relax, at least watch the process of your breathing, which automatically slows you down. Speak slower rather than faster and pitch your voice lower rather than higher.

Present ideas: well considered opinions are respected, even by people who do not agree with everything you say. When you can see how the land lies and a rapport has been established, you can start trialling ideas (e.g. your opinion of bricks-versus-clicks marketing, or whatever), but do check that you have their attention and that they want to listen. Remember to pause so that they can give you their prepared speeches.

Give and take: remember that they are looking to say yes, not no, so let them discover your qualities according to their own mindset. Don't try to impose ideas on them or hog the conversation, avoid being brash and boastful, and prepare for trick questions with modest and humorous answers (e.g. what is the worst mistake of your career and what is your worst fault?).

Ask for time: you are a mature person with commitments and a life – don't be rushed into agreeing anything and make it clear that you are seeking an advantageous career move. Bear in mind that they may also want more time for assessments, personality tests, etc, or just for consideration.

© Steven Holmes and John Peters. This section is licensed for publication by Monster. You can contact them for advice and assistance on *www.cvservices.net*.

_____ Great **expectations** _____

Different advisers will tell you different things about what the interview is ultimately for. Of course, it's for the employer to decide whether they want you or not, which is not always easy, even after an interview, but this is your concern: is the position right for you? What is the interview for from your perspective, and how should you approach it? Time for another three-part list:

☞ know

☞ show

☞ grow.

The first point has been covered already in a sense: know your stuff. This means knowing about:

☞ yourself

☞ your skills

☞ the job

☞ the company

☞ the field.

You can't know everything about any of these, and if you're moving into a completely new field for you, then it's all the more of a challenge, but surely you'll have done enough groundwork to know you want to be here, even if the actual job doesn't turn out to be for you (or you for it).[6] You're bound to learn more about it all in the course of being on the spot, but make sure you come across as being well informed from the start.

It's all very well to know things, but you've also got to show you know them which again means being focused and clear-headed. Don't be afraid to pause and think before answering, however: it's your honest answer they want, even if it's that you _don't_ know. Better to show that than bluff too hard and better to get the right job for you.

It's not just about knowledge, either, it's about showing yourself as a person. If you've

6 How can I find out? **page 115.**

been through elaborate psychometric tests, your potential employers may well have expectations in this direction, but regardless of that you should aim to answer honestly and in accordance with your real beliefs or knowledge on the subject. Take a look at the panel below for a reminder of the different stages of interviews.

_____ The five stages **of interviews** _____

☞ *Arriving*

Make sure you get there on time. It seems obvious, but so many people don't. Confirm your appointment beforehand by phone or e-mail. Smile and shake hands briefly and politely.

☞ *Behaving*

Speak clearly, and try to avoid just saying yes or no. Be natural, neither over-confident nor twitching in terror. Dress smartly but comfortably.

☞ *Answering*

Speak honestly. Admit it if you don't know the answer, but try to find the opportunity to sell yourself in other ways, and take your time.

☞ *Asking*

Don't ask questions when you already know the answer. Try to be interested in the goals of the company and how they relate to your own.

☞ *Leaving*

Be polite again, and smile if you still can. Make sure you know what the next step is – when will they contact you? Will there be a second round of interviews, etc?

Telephone **interviews**

Another possibility, especially if you're applying for a job abroad, is that you will be interviewed by telephone. Here are a few pointers:

☞ make sure you have any information you need to hand – company details, CV, etc;

> ☞ make sure you know who you're talking to, and remember there may be more than one person – keep them all in mind;
>
> ☞ banish distractions – disable call waiting if you use it, and make sure you won't be interrupted at home;
>
> ☞ express yourself – act natural, as if you were really there, and you will sound natural;
>
> ☞ confirm everything to show you've heard and understood – a 'yes' or 'thank you' keeps the flow of communication going.

You do need to know about the job, but never assume that an interview is going to be a dry exercise in testing your knowledge of it – that would be very unlikely. Ultimately the interview, for the employer, primarily represents their opportunity to suss you out as a person, whether you're friendly, flexible, imaginative, articulate, a team player or a lone wolf. Try to work out beforehand whether you know the answer to all these things yourself. Above all, don't be an automaton.

When it comes to your chance to ask questions, again you'll benefit from preparation. Often there'll be time at the end of the meeting for this, which career handbooks always assume, but what's wrong with asking questions when they're pertinent to whatever's being discussed? There's no reason why you shouldn't ask something when it occurs to you.

It's easy to assume you should be ready with dozens of questions about the job for when you're invited to turn the tables, but the best advice is to be more general, more focused on directions rather than positions. So in your preparation, don't just mindlessly write huge lists of questions soliciting data about the company, for example. A direction-focused approach means thinking about the context in which the company is located: how does it meet challenges within its ambit and from rivals? What are its goals? Often an employer will ask you something like 'Where do you see yourself in five years' time?'. You might well want to ask the same of the company.

_____ Virtually **got the job** _____

Most of the jobsites include content on the interview process as a matter of course, and if you've found one site in particular that appeals to you, you should read their advice, although beware: you could spend hours comparing what the different sites say and not be any the wiser.

Monster.co.uk has gone a step further: as part of its Career Centre, you can find a Virtual Interview. This offers a selection of typical interview questions, and you have to select which you think would be the best answer. Of course, there are no real 'right answers', but there are right ways of doing things.

Don't get too carried away with your own questions, however: at the end of the day, you are the one being interviewed, however much a 'meeting of minds' it might appear to be. And maybe keep a few ideas up your sleeve … there might still be a second round to get through.

Finally, there's 'grow'. Regardless of whether you get the job, every interview is a learning experience, and it's worth reflecting on it afterwards – not how well or how badly you did as such, but on how you approached it and how you might do it differently another time. Even if you get the job, the interview still offers a rich mine of experience to draw upon in other working situations; for one thing, you might soon be on the other side of the desk.

_____ Digitally **processed interviews** _____

Technology has made it possible for a halfway house between the normal interview and an entirely video-based one, and it's known as the digitally processed interview. In this case you will meet someone in person – the employer possibly, or maybe a recruitment agency acting on their behalf. They will record your responses to various questions and can then look at the material at their leisure.

There are various packages available in this arena. One is Screen-to-Screen's 'Intoview' software, which has been used by companies as diverse as Cap Gemini, Ford, and Tate & Lyle. It works by asking each candidate a set of identical questions, the responses to which are then processed into a computer presentation which can be sent to anyone involved in the recruitment process in the form of a CD ROM. An internet version is also available.

Another is Talking CV! from *www.isero.com*. Again, recruiters can mix and match from the responses they receive. 'The ability to publish "real-life" candidates on the internet is a tremendous breakthrough for online recruitment,' says managing director Stewart Keiller. 'Geographical barriers that have hampered the selection and short-listing process in the past need no longer be a problem.'

From your point of view, of course, the presence of a camera might not exactly help you to relax, but try to pretend it's not there. Always look at the interviewer rather than the camera, and follow the same advice as you would for any other interview.

What if you object to being filmed? Do you have any rights? Lawyer John Warchus sums it up: 'The interviewee certainly can refuse to have a recording done, but it isn't going to help his chances much.'

——— Distance **lends enchantment** ———

If you flick through the advertisements in a magazine like *Wired*, there are often pictures of people at work, but they're at home, or on a plane, or even on the beach. Just as employers and workers are beginning to embrace new ways of doing things, so the way they get together has to change. It's now perfectly possible to work somewhere far removed from your employer's headquarters.

A recent issue of the US digest of 'alternative culture', the *Utne Reader*, looked at modern ideas of being nomadic. In one feature, first published in the British magazine *Prospect*, Pico Iyer writes of his life as a 'postmodern riddle': he is of Asian origin with a British passport, lives with his girlfriend in Japan (and neither speaks more than a few words of the other's language) and works for an employer in New York.[7] He has to get up at 5am just to touch base with the team in the Big Apple: 'In our shrunken world, I can complete articles or even books without having to exchange a word with editors, and can draw money in a local department store from a bank account on the other side of the planet.'

 7 Tell me more about teleworking, **page 65.**

Now there's no reason why you can't seek, apply for, be tested and be interviewed for a job without meeting a single person in the flesh. In some cases this has already been done for some time, simply by using the telephone. A very busy employer might even resort to e-mail, or perhaps a private chatroom on the web.[8] Yet the technology now allows us to see each other, regardless of where we are.

Videoconferencing for interviews is still something of a novelty in Britain, although it has been used in the States for several years. Traditional recruiters are defensively saying that internet or remote recruitment will never replace face-to-face recruiting, but how true is that going to be when the internet offers employers as much convenience as it does jobseekers?

The costs of conducting a large recruitment campaign involving face-to-face interviewing can be enormous, particularly for an annual grouse hunt like the graduate milkround where dozens of posts might be up for grabs with a large employer. In addition to all the paperwork, whether or not it is handled by a dedicated human resources department, candidates often expect their travel expenses to be paid, and if there is a large programme of selection as well as interviewing, these costs can extend to hotel accommodation, too.

At the time of writing, there are reports in the news of London schools being so short of good teachers that they are turning to as far afield as Australia to recruit staff, but there can't be many headteachers who have either the funds or the time to go there in person. What better than a remote interview process that still enables face-to-face dialogue?

Going to interviews can also be an expensive business for you, the applicant. Not all firms are willing to fork out so generously for your expenses. Not only that, there is the cost in time off from work, from leisure ... and from applying for yet more jobs. Videoconferencing offers an obvious way of forestalling these problems, while retaining the advantages we all know of assessing people through being able to see them. The eyes have it.

However, few employers would take on someone without having met them, so if videoconferencing is to be used the tendency is to implement it for the first stage, as a weeding-out process. Candidates are then called to attend in person if they make it to the second round. If this is the case, there's all the more need to master the different media.

8 How do chatrooms work? **page 88.**

_____ Meeting **is cheating** _____

It used to be a joke that TV newsreaders aren't wearing any trousers – you can't see behind their desks. But even if you're sitting at home for an interview by webcam, you've got to take it seriously. And that means trousers.

Your seriousness should extend all the way to the top of your head, of course. An interview is an interview, and the limitations of videoconferencing, although they are basically few, mean that you have to pay even more attention to what is going on. Dress is still an issue, not only to convey the right impression but also to avoid turning yourself into an optical illusion: some patterns and hues are simply not suitable for reproduction via cathode ray tube. This doesn't mean that you have to get the BBC make-up department into your living room, but it does mean avoiding garish patterns.

_____ You're **on camera** _____

Some top tips for the videoconference interview:

- ☞ don't be intimidated – it's still just you and another person, discussing your suitability for the job;

- ☞ don't wear loud colours, especially bright whites, reds, black or strong patterns – they can spoil the picture. Avoid bright jewellery, too;

- ☞ be friendly – you won't have shaken hands with anyone, but you can still smile and look directly at the other person via the camera;

- ☞ try to keep fairly still, but without looking like you've seen Medusa's head;

- ☞ speak clearly, with a pause before answering questions.

The way you move on video is another significant factor. On the one hand, you need to avoid excessive fidgeting or moving about as you'll simply appear as a Superman blur rather than Superman. On the other hand, it's easy to appear too stiff, as many a football commentator bears witness. The main trick is to relax as if you were talking normally to someone in person, and to make sure that your voice and your image are your standard bearers. There's no room for nervous mumbling here.

You will therefore need to speak clearly and slowly, and one of the most important things is to wait for other people to finish speaking. Although video streaming across the internet or phone-based videoconferencing are improving in quality all the time, there is still a slight time lag in receiving both pictures and audio, much like transcontinental telephone calls. All you have to do is pause slightly before you respond – it will soon become natural. And don't let these little nuances make you dry up altogether.

Another issue is your surroundings. If the interview is to take place via dedicated videoconferencing equipment, you will almost certainly have to attend an office or recruitment consultancy premises, where this should be no problem: you should be seated in a quiet, undisturbed room. But it is possible to be interviewed at home, especially now that webcams and internet telephony are becoming so affordable, and if that's the case for you, it's vital that your drunk flatmates, small child or incontinent dog do not come wandering in.

Internet **telephony**

If you've had a terminal-to-terminal conversation with an employer, you might wonder whether you can do this at home. The answer is you can – and, as with e-mail, you can in theory talk to anyone in the world for the price of a local phone call, although the person at the other end will need the same equipment as you:

- a sound-equipped PC (i.e. with a good soundcard);
- a set of multimedia speakers;
- a microphone (although some computers, like the iMac, have one built in);
- suitable software, such as Microsoft's NetMeeting.

If you both have a webcam, you can even see who you're speaking to – NetMeeting can handle this, too. At the moment, it's not widely used, and don't expect pixel-perfect quality, but as bandwidth is improving all the time, it's bound to become more popular.

Other than these simple guidelines, and those shown in the panel, videoconferencing is easily absorbed as a new way of doing things, and the general advice on interview technique still applies. The game has rules, then, but it's important never to treat it too much like a game. Playing to win is important, but as always, it's the way you take part that really counts – and in this case, your future's at stake.

_____ What's **on offer?** _____

The time will come when you get a job offer, so should you accept it? Ask yourself the following questions, and use the net to help you find the answers:

☞ *Is it what you really want to do? Have you seen enough of the company, the workplace and the other staff to know you want to join them?*
If not, consider other jobs of course, but also consider trying to negotiate other ways of doing the one up for grabs. Would they let you work from home some of the time, for example? Or e-mail/telephone one of your interviewers; they might be able to clear up a few doubts for you.

☞ *Is the company going places, and going well?*
Nobody wants to start working for a company that's about to go down the tubes. Use the net to find out more about how well it's operating. Try its name in your favourite search engine, look it up on one of the newspapers' sites to find out what others say about it, and see if you can find a company report or the history of its share prices.

☞ *Does the salary meet your hopes and needs?*
Find out what other people in the same field are getting. At *www.totaljobs.co.uk*, for example, there's a 'salary checker' with details of current salaries in various jobs, while at *www.reed.co.uk* you can find out how much money you could get from relocating with its 'salary calculator'. Remember, too, that you must receive a proper contract to sign – it's now even possible for them to be sent digitally. If you've been led to expect a certain wage in an e-mail from the employer, keep it for future reference. E-lawyer John Warchus of Shadbolt & Co says: 'If the only correspondence you've got is e-mail, then that would be the evidence a court would use.'

☞ *Are you going to have to relocate*

Some of the main jobsites have articles with advice on relocation – look them up. And check out the area you might have to move to at *www.upmystreet.co.uk*. Issues such as house prices, nearest schools and even crime figures could affect your decision.

———————————————

You can always improve

Use the net to make the **most of your talents**

The message of the internet-savvy workplace is that there's

no excuse for resting on your laurels. If you've got the

dream job, don't just stop there

'There's only one corner of the universe you can be certain of improving, and that's your own self,' said Aldous Huxley.

If you've struggled through nearly 20 years of education and hated every minute of it, this aphorism may not strike you as particularly helpful, although self-improvement comes as much from experience as from education. But whether you're safely ensconced in a new job or making paper aeroplanes out of rejection letters, there are always ways to improve your skills. Needless to say, the internet offers a window on to many of them.

We've already seen the importance of keeping up to date in your chosen field of employment, particularly for career-changers, with a view to getting a new job.[1] But the message of the internet-savvy workplace is that there's no excuse for resting on your laurels. If you've got your dream job, don't just stop there.

1 Where I can find out more about a particular field? **Chapter 2.**

Regardless of whether you think your self needs improving, there are always ways to make the job you're in more rewarding – yes, more money and fewer hours are an obvious route, but enhancing your ability to do the job is just as important. Improving your skills is an obvious way to improve your chances of promotion within your present company, of getting a new job elsewhere, and generally of enhancing your workplace well-being. If you're working harder and enjoying what you're doing, everyone benefits.

Job satisfaction is a difficult thing to quantify at the best of times. A survey by the University of Warwick's economics department found that only 38 per cent of UK employees described themselves as being 'very satisfied' at work, while 14 per cent are actively 'dissatisfied'. The university's Professor Andrew Oswald calls this 'the curse of high aspirations': 'People with high levels of education appear to be much less easy to please than those with little formal education.' Adequate training, perhaps perceived by this group as a necessary follow-up to all those years of formal education, can certainly help.

The sad truth is that employers do not always provide adequate training for their staff. Sometimes they simply don't have the resources – but you do. You're bound to have come across some of them in your travels already, but here we are considering the resources of the internet with a slightly different aim in mind: not necessarily to help you find a new job, although the information here will always be relevant to that, but rather to help you make the most of the one you're in. And maybe you've just got a new one, so it's time to make the most of your enthusiasm.

_____ Follow **the light** _____

Before you consider specific training, you can benefit instantly and without effort simply by keeping up with what's new in your field. Let's recap on some of the ways in which you can do this:

-  checking web-based news or information services;
- joining industry bodies;
- reading magazines;
- going to conferences;
- using message boards and chatrooms;
- subscribing to mailing lists.

By now you've probably bookmarked several useful websites relevant to your work; if not, then it doesn't take long to do it. A few judicious minutes' use of a search engine can pull up plenty of useful services; all you have to do then is go to the Bookmarks or Favourites menu of your browser and add them to the list as you visit them one by one. If you want to narrow down the list later, it's easy to delete them (using 'Organize favourites', for example).[2]

Another idea is to set a page you've found to be useful and reliable as your 'home-page', so that it is the page that loads first when you fire up your browser software. It's amazing how many people never bother to change this, which in part explains the hit counts that Microsoft gets. It takes a matter of moments to go to the preferences or options setting in your browser's menus to set a different homepage. This way you could set up a useful news service (maybe just the general news somewhere like *www.bbc.co.uk*) to appear when you start work every day so you can scan the headlines before getting on with the day's tasks.

A lot of companies with continuous internet access have the company's own site set as everyone's homepage, but why? Unless this site has a vital newsfeed, it's hardly going to tell you anything you don't already know.

Another good idea is to set your favourite search engine as a homepage. Most browsers have a 'search button' at the top which you can use, and this can often be con-figured to go to the search tool of your choice rather than the one that Microsoft or Netscape prefer (i.e. probably have a huge sponsorship deal with). Search is often the most common activity on the net, and if you use it primarily as a research tool for a wide variety of areas, you might as well set the search engine as your homepage. It's surpris-ing how lazy little details like this can make a difference to your day.

Speaking of 'newsfeeds', sometimes sites have a special scrolling 'ticker tape' of news stories which roll across your screen somewhere like underground train indicators – except in this case they usually work. If you resize your browser window so that it just shows this bit, it can be a useful and unobtrusive way of keeping up with news as it breaks, but without cluttering your screen with distracting browser windows. Check out *www.newsindex.com* for some examples.

Joining an industry body ought to keep you up to date.[3] Most publish regular newslet-ters, and many are now doing the same on the web. Again, reading the relevant trade

2 Tell me about expert search techniques, **page 22.**
3 How can I find these? **page 21.**

magazines is a great way to keep in touch with what's going on.[4] If you can find one that puts its news stories on the web, then even better – that way you can avoid amassing huge piles of old issues all over your office which you then ritually purge every few years. If there isn't a 'News' link on the homepage of your favourite trade body or magazine's website, move on to an alternative.

The national newspapers are always worth a look, too.[5] With some, not only can you search their archives for relevant stories but you can subscribe to particular channels to receive stories that match certain criteria. It's essentially the same process as setting up job search agents. Being lazy, after all, is a sign of sophistication – although it's not recommended that you say that in an interview.

Using the **net at work**

If you've got fast internet access at work, it's very tempting to make the most of it for jobsearching and gleaning information. Lots of people are doing it: one financial recruitment site, *www.doublecuff.com*, has published a survey showing that 70 per cent of visits to its site occur in the working week – although not at lunchtime. But you may be being watched – the owners of digital TV channel Jobchannel.tv, MMTV, found in their research that 76 per cent of jobseekers were aware of their employers monitoring their use of the web, so they preferred to surf at home.

Here's what e-law expert John Warchus of Shadbolt & Co (*www.shadboltlaw.co.uk*) has to say: 'Using facilities at work can be a bit problematic. It's all a bit fluid at the moment, given one or two legal changes in the air, but there have been cases where people have been dismissed for spending too much time on the computer at work. One quite well-known case involved a lady who spent a lot of time looking for a holiday. A lot will depend on the individual company's IT policy and e-mail policy. A serious breach of an IT policy can lead to dismissal.'

4 And what about these? **page 21, page 62.**
5 Such as? **pages 20–21.**

Oh, and if you have been surfing at work and don't want it to be blatantly obvious what you've been up to to the next person who sits at your desk, go directly to the preferences/options of your browser and clear out (a) the history, (b) the cookies[6], (c) the cache.[7] Be warned, though, that even when a hard drive has been completely wiped, data can still be recovered …

——— Talking **shop** ———

Another sure sign that you've really got sucked into your job – hopefully for the better – is going to conferences. For all the charms that free hotel accommodation and entertainment by an Alan Partridge lookalike offer, hopefully there are speakers who really know what they're talking about and can impart it to you rewardingly. Good use of a search engine should help you turf up conferences in your field, and again, niche sector sites can help.[8] Conferences are often organised by the same people who publish trade magazines. To return to an example from an earlier chapter, *www.careinfo.org* is run by a specialist medical publisher. Look through the site, and there's a page dedicated to conferences. Try *www.exhibitions.co.uk* for details of industry events across the whole gamut of sectors.

There's also a good chance that if you've missed a conference you might be able to find copies of the speakers' papers archived online, although somebody out there is usually trying to make money from running events like this, so you might not find it all for free. Here's an idea, though: find out from the web a list of the speakers' names, and you can then run a search for *them*. That way you might well find other papers by them, books to read, websites they run, perhaps an e-mail address you could use to contact them personally for information. Never be afraid to use an e-mail address you've found: if it's advertised, they must expect people to be getting in touch.

Which brings us back to meeting people 'in person, far away'. By the same token that

6 I'm sorry? **page 86.**
7 And what's that? **page 77.**
8 Any tips on finding these? **page 62.**

people who publish their e-mail address must expect to receive e-mails,[9] so anyone who is 'appearing' in a special chat session,[10] say, or who offers to answer questions posed to a bulletin board,[11] is there to respond. Ask and the answer shall be given unto you – or at least they could point you to some place where it might be.

But perhaps the most useful means of 'keeping up' is the mailing list.[12] There really is a mailing list for every subject, and the advantage of these is that you can read them at your leisure, or not at all. You can often choose the amount of information you receive: recall the 'digest' facility explained in Chapter 5.[13]

The most helpful mailing list messages commence with a pithy list of 'headlines'. You can then scan these quickly and see if it's worth your while reading the full stories further down. If not, just hit the delete key in your e-mail program and you can get on with something else.

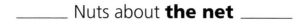

Nuts about **the net**

Hitting the delete key begins to take on a new significance if you've signed up to more than a couple of mailing lists or, in some cases, even only one. If you don't keep a wary eye on your inbox, you can amass hundreds of messages in no time. With this in mind, daily mailing lists are best avoided – go for a fortnight's holiday and there'll be floods on your desktop when you return. Some mailing lists actually allow you to send a special message to say you're going to be away so they don't need to send you any messages – check the FAQ. It's the online equivalent of a note to your milkman.

This raises the whole issue of keeping your messages and web bookmarks organised. As suggested above, you can use your browser's options to tidy up lists of favourite websites, and these can be placed into a user-defined folder. E-mail programs generally offer the same sort of facility, but with even greater functionality.

Once you've started embracing the internet into your daily routines, the messages really do build up, and sometimes you'll want to squirrel away the tastiest nuts. The first thing to do is set up a range of subfolders inside your inbox (this is the terminology of

9 How else can I find e-mail addresses? **page 27.**
10 Where can I find out more about online chat? **page 88.**
11 How do these work? **page 74.**
12 How do mailing lists operate? **page 83.**
13 What does this mean? **page 85.**

Outlook Express here, as that's by far the most likely e-mail program you'll be using, but the general principles should apply to other programs such as Eudora). You can now choose to drag individual messages – or groups of them, by shift- or control-clicking – from the main inbox where they first appear to the appropriate subfolder.[14] It's also a good way to keep 'business' and 'personal' messages apart, although you're still recommended to use different e-mail addresses altogether.

This is all very well, but nobody likes housekeeping very much, and this sort of admin is hardly exciting. There's a solution, however, that enables you to automate much of this tidying up. In Outlook Express you can set up things known as mail 'rules'. These are logical statements applied against every incoming message and sometimes leading to an appropriate action. For example, you can set them up so that every time you get an e-mail message from *mum@home.com*, it will be moved into the 'Lectures' folder.

The point is that you can now let the program file your messages before you even read them, and you can then see how many new messages there are in each folder at a glance in the same way that you knew there were X messages in your inbox before you set all this up.

Mail rules can analyse the address of the sender and what they type into the subject line, and can even look for words in the body of the message. So every time someone writes to you about the Widget 8000, the messages can be kept together by theme. Mail rules aren't perfect, however. If you want every e-mail with the name 'Sue' in the subject line to go to the 'Sue' folder, don't be surprised if a few rogues appear – messages with the word 'issue' in them, for example. It takes a little practice refining the rules, but they're a very powerful tool. You can even set up rules to reply to messages automatically, although you should be more careful with this, or the wrong message could be sent out to the wrong person.

14 Tell me more about this, **page 39.**

_____ Processed **junk** _____

Using mail rules to filter messages raises another issue: junk mail, or spam.[15] How can you stop those tedious 'offers' clogging your inbox? The short answer is that you can't, but there are a few things to reduce it significantly:

☞ note down any common domain names from which spam seems to appear, and set up a mail rule to delete all mail that comes from them;

☞ see if your e-mail program has a blocking facility: some webmail servers, such as Hotmail, allow you to create lists of e-mail addresses which you don't ever want to hear from again;[16]

☞ set up more than one e-mail address and use a proper POP3 account for serious use, and a webmail one which you don't care about;

☞ use an alias on newsgroups, i.e. don't put your real return e-mail address in when you set up your newsreader.

One thing you should **not** do is reply to the spammer, even if you've been given an address to 'unsubscribe' to. All it means is that they know yours is a real, active e-mail address, and they'll probably spam you even more.

_____ Trouble **in store** _____

This issue of 'information overload' does not just apply to e-mail. The chances are that if you are starting to surf the net on a daily basis, you will want to save information for future reference – the pages _might_ still be there online in perpetuity, but the cruel truth of the net is that things change all the time, and even if you stored a bookmark only last month, you can easily find that the site is no longer available, or has been relaunched, or simply purged of some of its material in order to avoid paying for more server space.

It's worth picking up a few tricks, therefore, about storing data for future reference. In the case of e-mail, you can obviously save individual messages; unfortunately not all

15 When am I at risk from spam? **page 88.**
16 What's the difference between POP3 and webmail? **page 79.**

programs allow you to save entire sets of them. There is a way round this, however. All you need to do is track down the 'inbox' file or folder (or its equivalent) on your hard drive and you can then back that up somewhere by copying it.

As for websites, there are various ways in which you can save them: Internet Explorer offers three choices – plain text, HTML, or something called a web archive. Netscape offers equivalents.

If the information you want to save is very much text-based and will suffice without all the flashy graphics that no doubt vie for your attention around its periphery, you can just choose text. If that text includes various links to other sites, you are better off saving in HTML: this means that you can double-click on the file later on and it will open up in your browser; you can then click on those links if you want to follow them up, or simply read the text off-line.

Finally, there's the web archive option. What this does is calculate all the elements that make up the entire page, text and graphics alike; the browser then downloads them all and compresses them into one file. It's very handy – Explorer now offers the option to save an 'HTML archive' which will do the same but preserves all the individual files as separate elements. There's probably no point in you doing this, as you can still extract individual elements of a (more memory-efficient) web archive after you've opened it. You do this by clicking the right mouse button (PCs) or holding down the button (Macs) over the particular page element you want to play with.

These technicalities are a little by the by. The point is that you can preserve an entire web page for future reference – or even an entire website if you have (a) an 'off-line browser' program and (b) the patience.[17]

If you're going to do this sort of thing a lot, you might want to invest in a storage medium such as a Zip drive or a CD writer, both to save your hard drive space (although with the present capacities of new machines available, this may not be an issue) and to give you your data in a more portable format – so you can take it home from work, for example.

This book is not the place for great swathes of technical details, but suffice it to say that an average web page in plain text or HTML format is unlikely to take up more than about 50K, and a web archive probably not more than 250K, depending on the graphics involved. The internet is generally a memory-friendly medium, as the bigger the graphics, the longer it takes for a page to load, and people will just clear off elsewhere. This impatient world is usually to your advantage.

17 Tell me about off-line browsing, **page 77.**

A normal floppy disk will hold just under 1.5Mb of data; a Zip cartridge 100Mb; and a CD more than 600Mb. All this means that you can often get an entire website on to just one floppy (most sites average less than 10Mb overall, and 100Mb is huge – not that this means they don't come any bigger), and a single CD can store literally thousands of sites, graphics and all. To invoke a common comparison, a book of this length takes up less than 1Mb of disk space (considerably less if suitable compression techniques are used); so one CD can store an entire multi-volume encyclopedia. These media are cheap, so it really is easy to keep all this data.

One caveat on this theme: despite their prevalence, you are counselled against using floppy disks. It is a dying technology, and many new computers (such as Apple's iMacs) don't come with a floppy drive any more. Floppies don't have a very good shelf life either, so use another medium if you can, unless it's something unimportant or relatively ephemeral.

There is one other way of storing data worth mentioning, and that's on the internet itself. There are various ways in which this can work. One is to use a web-based archiving service – this enables you to upload huge amounts of data. At *www.data-archive.co.uk*, there's a specialised archive for education and training materials. You could even sign up with a free ISP and you'll often get 10Mb or considerably more to use for your own purposes, which could include storage of files. This does not mean that the world and its significant other can see what you've stored, however; if you don't publicise it, nobody's going to know (and you can have pages that are not connected to any others), although security is always going to be an issue on the web.[18]

If you'd still like to keep life simple and stick to a bookmark-based filing system, you could also set up a weblog.[19] Finally, never discount the value of e-mailing things to yourself from one address to another (your work one to your home one, for example) – it's a great way of backing things up so that they're always to hand.[20]

18 Am I at risk from viruses? **page 86.**
19 What is a weblog exactly? **pages 57–58.**
20 Tell me about different types of e-mail, **page 79.**

⎯⎯⎯ Drowning **in data?** ⎯⎯⎯

Research by recruitment consultancy Schofield Hughes has revealed that an average of 120 e-mails are received every day by 7 million users in the UK alone. Even just surfing the web for half an hour can lead to a kind of *weltschmerz* unique to the net. Tom Campbell, internet expert and futurologist from the new media think-tank New Media Knowledge (*www.nmk.co.uk*) offers some advice on scything through the chaff: 'Information overload is not a new phenomenon. In fact, it was first recognised by 19th-century businessmen in the age of the telegraph. A few tips I would suggest are:

☞ limit your information portals to just a few at a time, although always be prepared to change and update these sources;

☞ don't get panicked into thinking you're missing something, or that the really valuable stuff is elsewhere. If you find yourself spending more of your time consuming information than actually using it, then something is probably wrong;

☞ it helps to print out large amounts of information and take short notes rather than passively surfing through lots of screen information, which can often make you feel a bit disorientated and lost.'

⎯⎯⎯ Centres **of excellence** ⎯⎯⎯

This techie stuff is all very well, but you've got to have stuff you want to save, which brings us back to the theme of improving yourself. If you're serious about learning new skills for the workplace (or for your own enjoyment, for that matter), the world of online training offers a wealth of new opportunities. There are two main routes you can take:

☞ DIY

☞ WBT.

DIY, oddly enough, means 'do it yourself'. With well-developed search skills, there's no reason why you can't find out almost anything on the net. The whole shebang first took off from its military origins through being adopted by academia as a means of sharing knowledge, and that knowledge is often (though not always) accessible to everyone. If your area of interest or need is covered by a specific university course, for example, the chances are that that university has put a load of resources online for its official students to use, and you can often get at them too – it's like wandering into a lecture hall when you're technically not supposed to be there.

Beyond this, you can simply trawl the web at large for data of interest to you, and treat it all as your own personalised training course. But the world of employment is notoriously snooty about unquantified intellectual experience, and the chances are that gaining a real qualification of some kind will impress people more, even if you've learned less getting it, and that's where web-based training (WBT) comes in.

A report by the International Data Corporation (IDC) asked an important question in its title: *Online vs On-site: To what extent can live instruction be replaced?* The report showed that web-based learning is set to become a major player in the next few years and is increasingly attractive to both employers and employees. Its advantages include:

- ☞ training whenever you need it;
- ☞ almost infinite flexibility of course elements;
- ☞ accessibility from anywhere;
- ☞ no need to stop normal work;
- ☞ instruction content remains the same.

In other words, you know you can get the knowledge and experience you need whenever and wherever it's convenient, and you won't have your time wasted when the lecturer arrives with a hangover. So how does all this work?

There are some 'courses' you can find on the net which are free, and in America there are various 'online universities' which claim to offer one-to-one 'tuition' in this way – as ever, these will be the sites that rely upon advertising, and you may well question the origin of their 'expertise'. If it's free, you can probably find it for yourself, with more freedom to pick and choose. Having said that, there are many selfless sites on the web that really do offer valuable training, particularly in fields such as web design; in other words, if you want to work in the internet world, there's no better place to go than the net itself, and you can find it for free.

Increasingly, though, more serious and formalised sites are growing up, which offer a structured course, with real access to real people as tutors, and even real qualifications at the end of it. One such site is *www.ilearn.to*, which has forged a partnership with the Department for Education and Employment. The idea is that you can log into your own dedicated web space, where you can receive modules of instruction. Often there are 'simulations' available, i.e. interactive sessions or presentations that demonstrate a particular skill in action. There are also online questionnaires and tests to do, and at the end of it (in some cases) you can receive recognised accreditation. All this comes at a price, but there are various ways to pay for your training – and more than 400 courses available to date. These are often workplace-orientated, such as Time Management, Customer Service or Office 2000.

Another player in this field is KnowledgePool (*http://eu.knowledgepool.com*). This site offers 'online mentor support', for example, whereby you can enter a live chatroom to communicate both with your tutor and fellow students. Many sites also contain 'libraries' of questions and answers that relate to common enquiries. KnowledgePool claims that a personal tutor can answer your queries by e-mail within a maximum of six hours.

Some of the jobsites have hooked up to online trainers. *www.fish4jobs.co.uk*, for example, has a partnership with online trainer blueU.com. High street recruiter Manpower has set up its own Global Learning Centre, at *www.manpoweronline.net*, with around 1 500 courses available, some of them free.

_____ Keeping **your grip** _____

Is online training for you? If it's of genuine quality and affordable (or paid for by your firm), there's really no good reason why not, and you might well find it vastly preferable to the way in which you've learned things in the past. One of the standard criticisms of 'distance learning' of all kinds is that you lose out in terms of personal contact, but if you want to learn and there are people you can communicate with via e-mail or in live chat-rooms, are you really missing out?[21] The technology is already here for videoconferenced seminars, so you can even see the people you're studying 'with'.[22] It seems that this is one area where employers really are embracing technology anyway: it's in their

---

21 Where can I find relevant chatrooms? **page 88.**
22 Tell me about videoconferenced interviews, **pages 130–134.**

own interests to keep their staff onsite, yet with full training facilities available, often cheaply.

Nevertheless, it may still be the case that you want a more 'traditional' qualification: a full-blown degree, perhaps, in a year out from work or studied part-time. As ever, the internet can still help, and so we come full circle to using it as a research tool.

If you point your browser to *www.stepstone.com*, for example, you can follow a link to 'education and training'. Here there lurks a searchable database of courses of all kinds offered at both academic and vocational institutions across the country. You can follow links to the organisations which offer the courses and find out more from them. There can be few educational institutions nowadays that don't put their prospectuses online in some form at least, and even if they don't, they should offer useful contact details. The Open University (*www.open.ac.uk*) lets you fill in a form to receive by post whichever prospectuses you require.

Wellbeing **at work**

When Huxley wrote his maxim about self-improvement, he was probably not simply referring to education. The net clearly offers excellent routes to intellectual, and maybe even practical, self-advancement, but there remain more nebulous areas where self-improvement or self-care come in.

Keeping your grip on your job does not just mean developing new skills and staying a step ahead of your rivals; it also means managing the effects of work on you and your personal life. If you're making a career change, for example, it can be overwhelming or confusing; or there may be relocation issues within your company.[23] These are factors that affect your life outside the workplace as well as within it.

One such factor is stress. Stress can debilitate, destroy, confuse, even kill with its consequences. Stress management is a vital area in your career, and it's no accident that some of the jobsites have stress counsellors available online. One of Monster's experts is one, and you can e-mail him with questions about stress in the workplace.

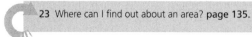

23 Where can I find out about an area? **page 135.**

_____ Beating **stress** _____

Stress in the workplace is costing British businesses millions every day – according to the Confederation of British Industry (CBI), it works out at around £12 billion a year – but more important still is the cost it exacts on people's lives. Everyone's situation is different, but here are a few watchwords for the wary:

☞ know yourself and what makes you stressed, and try to avoid jobs where those situations might arise;[24]

☞ manage your time carefully – plan tasks ahead, and don't take on too much;

☞ communicate – if you've got too much on your plate, tell your employer;

☞ don't take work home with you – complete your tasks and call it a day;

☞ take breaks – don't spend every lunchtime at your desk with a sandwich.

If stress has become too much a part of your life, have a look at _www.stress.org.uk_ for resources and information.

The internet offers huge resources for support and counselling as well as the more obvious self-development tools. Some of them may seem over-indulgent or navel-gazing, but until you've experienced stress, you may not appreciate their value. The message is that you can always improve – but don't let it happen at too high a price. Even using the internet itself too much can be a cause of stress …

24 Can the internet help with this? **page 115.**

Use your **resources**

There are many wider workplace issues where the internet can help.

☞ Equal opportunities – ask an expert at *www.monster.co.uk*, and read up on the law at *www.equalops.co.uk*.[25]

☞ Employment law – you can find some useful links at *www.emplaw.co.uk*.[26]

☞ Sexual harassment – visit the Citizens' Advice Bureaux site at *www.adviceguide.org*.

☞ Privacy[27] and security[28] issues – read the relevant sections in this book.

☞ Health and safety – the official Health and Safety Executive site is at *www.hse.gov.uk*.

Finally, there's an excellent, entertaining, disturbing and informative site run by the BBC, called Workers at War. At *www.bbc.co.uk/education/war*, it includes links to many useful resources for workplace issues.

---

25 How do I contact an expert? **page 74.**
26 What other legal issues do I need to know about? **page 87, page 103, page 118.**
27 Am I being watched? **page 88, page 140.**
28 Is my personal data safe? **page 87.**

CHAPTER TEN

Striving and arriving

The internet **unravelled**

The advantage modern technology has given us over our forebears is that new ways of marshalling our time and resources are opening up to us

The vision of the future presented in 1950s and 1960s science fiction movies often looks slightly ridiculous to us. As often as not, we are all wearing outlandish metallic clothing as we travel in our metallic personal spacepods and rehydrate our metallic concentrated food tablets. Ours is a life of leisure, where everyday chores are carried out by robots and all we have to do is sit around sipping bright purple drinks and playing three-dimensional chess.

This hasn't happened – and yet it has. Although the world we live in is as gritty and smelly and confusing as it probably always will be, it's surprising how many of these 21st-century visions are actually with us. Because change happens around us all the time, it's often difficult to see.

Wander into one of the new Tube stations on London's extended Jubilee Line, for example, and you are greeted by huge metallic chambers, cathedrals of our time perhaps, where the individual is dwarfed by the technology that has been used to create them. Wander along Oxford Street or Tottenham Court Road, and you can while away an hour in an internet café where hundreds of others sit beside you, row by row, checking their e-mail, looking for jobs, researching, shopping just like you are. Then walk a few doors down and you can pop into an express supermarket, where you can buy a ready-made meal to heat and eat in minutes. It's often just a matter of how you look at things.

We don't lead lives of leisure, and there are many good reasons why we shouldn't, but the advantage modern technology has given us over our forebears is that new ways of marshalling our time and resources are opening up to us. The internet is a major part of that social change.

Yet even after a good five years of established use in this country (many more if you're in academia, say, or are the head of MI5), many people remain distrustful of the net, for a variety of reasons, and in all walks of life there are those who resist its advances and warn of its dangers. All technology has dangers – but only if it's misused, or people who aren't willing to understand it react against it.

By the time you've read this far, you'll almost certainly have used the internet to a considerable extent, if you hadn't already beforehand. Specifically, you will probably have used it to help you look for a job, or at least to suss out the opportunities that are available to you. Hopefully you will have found it a rewarding activity. But you may still have a few lingering doubts, or others have suggested them to you. Is the internet really the way ahead or is it merely a flash in the pan, waiting to be replaced by something else equally faddish?

There can't be a definitive answer to that question, although the evidence suggests that it is both here to stay, albeit in ever-evolving forms, and here to help. But let's try to answer some of those doubts.

> **"Ultimately, I think the internet will become the primary means of advertising and looking for work. The enormous size of the audience and specificity of positions that it offers makes traditional media forms (e.g. newspapers) seem obsolete and vastly overpriced."**
>
> Tom Campbell, futurologist, New Media Knowledge

_____ Don't shoot **the messenger** _____

Users and abusers of the internet alike can easily develop misunderstandings as to what it does, how it works, and who is using it. So in this final chapter, here are answers to some of the most common criticisms levelled at it from the perspective of using the net to find a job or enhance your career.

☞ *Employers are not really that keen on using the net for recruitment*

The evidence suggests otherwise. Various surveys indicate that between half and three-quarters of employers in the UK are already using the internet as part of their recruitment strategy. Even if the company you want to work for doesn't appear to be among them, or still hasn't got beyond brochureware, they almost certainly will – and soon, if they want to thrive.

It's being led by demand. Although internet shopping has still not taken off in a big way, internet jobhunting has – that's why you're here. Research by *www.work-thing.com* in 2000 revealed that 31 per cent of internet users had looked at job opportunities, representing around 4 million people in the UK alone. A further 4 million were expected to use the net as part of their career strategy as soon as they wanted to look for a new job. Andrew Grant, CEO (Europe) of TMP Executive Resourcing, has gone on record as saying that 'there will be over 100 million CVs on the internet this decade'.

Employers will always be keen on finding the best candidates, and if almost every graduate is looking online, you can be sure they'll have lined up in cyberspace to meet them.

☞ *It's not easy to find the best jobs on the internet*

Anyone who has registered with one of the jobsites is likely to have experienced a certain amount of frustration, it's true. Not with the way the sites themselves work, but with the responses they get – one day you'll get details of two jobs e-mailed to you, the next it might be 200. Some of them you saw last week; many will be totally wide of the mark anyway. There are ways to improve the accuracy of the results you get – that's what Chapter 3 of this book is all about – but no system is perfect.

Yet stop and think about how things were before and how they are now – they're not perfect, but they're a damned site better. Ben Giddings of Monster.co.uk puts it in perspective: 'Every Monday, thousands of people buy the *Guardian* looking for media, marketing and sales jobs. Every Monday, your average person will see about four at most that are suitable. And sometimes none at all. Out of about 40 pages! Yet the *Guardian* is lauded as one of the best national recruitment papers in the country.

'What a lot of people fail to realise is that a website doesn't give *better* jobs, it gives better, faster, more convenient *access* to a greater range of jobs; it makes applying for them easier and faster; and it gives you access to far more information concerning both the companies and the marketplaces in which they operate. It therefore strengthens the candidate's position and gives them better resources. But it doesn't make the vacancies themselves any better.

'Put it this way. You go into a library, look through the shelves, scan a few catalogues, ask an assistant, and finally find a copy of JR Hartley's *Fly Fishing*. You go on the web, type in the title and ten seconds later you have 200 links detailing every site that even mentions the book … But it doesn't make the book any better to read.'

Whether the book is worth reading or the job worth applying for is always going to be down to you – and you wouldn't want it any other way.

☞ *The internet is too broad and chaotic a medium*
The very breadth of the internet is one of its strengths, but it can come at a price. The limitless and ever-growing amount of material in cyberspace can be overwhelming, and it might seem that you cannot have any guarantee of finding who or what you're looking for. You could say the same of the real world, though – and the real world lacks the benefit of cleverly organised search engines.

Again, demand from users like you is helping to shape the internet into what people really want. It's important that demand does indeed come from individual users rather than huge corporations, which is why the internet has a huge ethical advantage over a 'push' medium like television, however much the big advertisers are trying to take it over.

☞ *The internet is destroying the coherence of society*
Telework guru Gil Gordon, writing from America where the net has far more of a cultural hold than it does in the UK as yet, is keen to put the internet in context: it is as much a subject of change as it is a driving force for it: 'I think that the internet has played a big role but would not say that it, or any other aspect of technology, has driven telework. The underlying factors have more to do with the trends in

decentralising the traditional centralised office, changes in employee preferences and values, and employer pressures to cut operating expenses.

'Despite the wonders of the internet, there are still other factors that account for interest in and success with telework, e.g. managerial attitudes, proper training, proper policies, good selection of tasks and workers, and much more. Thus, the internet is best viewed as a very powerful catalyst, but nothing more.'

Gil Gordon's comments apply to the internet's role in education, economics and communication every bit as much as telework: it's a catalyst, but it's part of a wider flow of change in society. Symptomatic of it, yes, but responsible for it, no. Shaping the world around us is, after all, an inherently collective responsibility.

You can do absolutely anything on the internet

This is as much a misunderstanding as saying that there are things you *can't* do on the net. It's a pathway, not a panacea. Back to the first point: some of it has to be down to you. Ben Giddings again: 'No matter how much the promoters bang on about personalisation, etc, the web does not think for you. So you still have to apply time and thought into how you use what is essentially a highly sophisticated database/library.

'I think the main problem though is that people have overrated expectations of the internet. They are used to hearing that it gets you into a global network of information and therefore jump to the conclusion that a job website will give you access to every job that is out there. I don't think some people understand that we operate in the same way as a newspaper, getting companies to post job adverts, not globally accessing every vacancy in the world!'

The time may well come when every vacancy in the world is accessible – but it will still be up to you to find them, and the more choice you have as you follow that quest, the better. However, the jobs can only come to you if you're the right person, and it's precisely by making the effort to demonstrate this that you deserve them.

The internet cannot offer the same service that traditional agencies do

At the time of writing there is a huge debate raging between the online recruiters and those resolute in staying off-line – but the Luddites will lose out. Recruiters complain that the internet cannot possibly replace the face-to-face approach, although, as you'll have seen in this book, technology is more than sophisticated enough to mean that people don't have to be in the same room to meet.

Another complaint is that online recruiters don't know enough about their markets. In some cases, this is probably true – the fast and flashy start-ups which promise the earth but don't have the real market knowledge to follow through. When dozens of jobsites are vying for your attention, how do you know which ones are the best? This book has given you some pointers, but the proof of the pudding is in who asks for seconds: if you find a site works for you, you'll go back to it. It's not hard to try a few out and see which work.

Inevitably, as a new way of doing business becomes available, some people seek to exploit it. But others seek to regulate. In the UK, the government is already clamping down on bad practice in the recruitment industry, and that includes anyone recruiting online. There is also an Association of Online Recruiters (AOLR), which has been recognised by the official body of the recruitment industry, the Recruitment and Employment Confederation (REC). Good standards will prevail.

And as David Brown, managing director of *www.gisajob.com*, points out: 'By using a recruitment site, candidates *are* using agencies … thousands of them. People want the biggest bang for their buck … and if they can submit one CV and it ends up on the desk of the top agencies the next day, then why not!?'

⎯⎯⎯ Don't just do something: **sit there** ⎯⎯⎯

According to Forrester Research, by 2005 global career networks are likely to have captured 55 per cent of the global online recruitment market. Jeff Taylor, CEO of Monster.com, has expressed his hope that in a few years' time there will be only a couple of 'resume tanks' in the whole world – that the monsters will have swallowed the minnows.

Time will tell, and from your point of view, however effective those sites become, diversity remains important. Although the diversity of the internet can overwhelm, it also means that somewhere out there you can almost always find a product, service or community that makes you feel at home, and that's what you are looking for.

The big jobsites have taken a strong lead in creating that sense of home, but sometimes you want to visit the cornershop instead of the hypermarket. And sometimes, as a jobseeker, you might not want to use the internet at all. Nobody is saying that it's the only way to do things, however effective it is. The only real way to get ahead is to try things and see if they work for you.

"If you want fast access to a lot of jobs, the ability to research companies, the ability to apply online, quick (if not always perfectly accurate) search facilities, and you're in an industry that is quite well represented online, then go for it. If you are in a profession where networking, personal contact, or traditional attitudes are dominant, perhaps you're best off elsewhere. It all comes down to the individual. The *Guardian* is an excellent recruitment paper, but it's not right for everyone. How do you know if it's right for you? Read it. Same with the web."

Ben Giddings, content manager, Monster.co.uk

Index